DATE LIKE A WOMAN

KAI NICOLE

FLAIMAHMY PRESS
PACIFICA, CA

COPYRIGHT (C) FEBRUARY 2017
BY KAI NICOLE

ALL RIGHTS RESERVED

NO PART OF THIS BOOK MAY BE REPRODUCED IN ANY MANNER WHATSOEVER WITHOUT WRITTEN
PERMISSION EXCEPT IN THE CASE OF BRIEF QUOTATIONS USED IN ARTICLES AND REVIEWS

PUBLISHED IN THE UNITED STATES BY

FLAIMAHMY PRESS

WWW.FLAIMAHMY.CO

LIBRARY OF CONGRESS CONTROL NUMBER: 2017937636
NICOLE, KAI
DATE LIKE A WOMAN
KAI NICOLE ———— 1ST ED

ISBN 978-0-692-86435-7
PRINTED IN THE UNITED STATES OF AMERICA
COVER DESIGN BY LARMARROUS SHIRLEY
10 9 8 7 6 5 4 3 2 1

WHEN IT COMES TO DATING, WOMEN IN GENERAL HAVE A LOT OF OUTLANDISH EXPECTATIONS... BUT, [T]HE NUMBER OF MALE "DATING GURUS" WHO SPOUT THE MOST SEXIST DATING DRIVEL HAS SOMEHOW SKYROCKETED IN POPULARITY.

MY GOAL IN [DATE LIKE A WOMAN] IS TO HELP WOMEN END UNREALISTIC EXPECTATIONS IN DATING AND REPLACE THEM WITH NEW REALISTIC ONES.

I HOPE TO HELP MANY WOMEN FREE THEIR MINDS FROM SEXIST DATING EXPECTATIONS AND SEXISM IN GENERAL. I ALSO HOPE TO HELP WOMEN UNDERSTAND THAT MY UNCONVENTIONAL APPROACH TO DATING WILL ALLOW THEM TO LEARN ABOUT THEMSELVES, HAVE A MORE SUCCESSFUL DATING LIFE, ENJOY THE ART OF DATING, AND JUST BE HAPPIER IN GENERAL.

FIRST PAPERBACK EDITION

Contents

INTRODUCTION

To be honest, Twitter. Twitter made me want to write this book. If you are a participant on Twitter you understand its value in terms of social commentary. The hot topics of the moment are always shared and discussed on Twitter allowing anyone who participates in the discussion to gain insight into what people in general are thinking. Relationships, dating, men and women, are often discussed. Plus, one of my Twitter followers encouraged me to do so. That's what got me started three years ago.

Outside of sharing my dating tips with my closest girlfriends, I usually never tell others how I approach dating. I think that I have always approached dating differently from other women. Not that I follow any arbitrary rules, however, I do not think I have always known that my thoughts about dating were as far outside the norm as they are. Over the years, after speaking with many different women and men, I came to realize that my personality, my upbringing, my personal approach to life left me in a space of mental freedom that many women who have been indoctrinated in our culture and sexism, have never had the opportunity to feel.

Despite my unconventional dating beliefs, (which is why I've probably kept them to myself), I have been quite a successful dater. Most of the time men have wanted serious relationships with me after going out just a few times. My single life has always been brief stints between long-term relationships. Basically, it's hard for me to stay single; offers of relationships come quickly for me. If you are wondering if I have ever been married, which is usually the "proof" that you've been "successful" at dating, the answer is "yes." I've had three long-term relationships each lasting anywhere from three to nine years. I know how to date. Trust me on this. And, before you point out my three serious relationships over 20 years as some sort of failure, let me emphasize that this is a book about learning to date, not a relationship guide; I know how to date. Relationships are a whole different topic. Maybe one day I will write a book about them, but for now I want to pass on some knowledge I have found to be very helpful about dating.

Whenever perusing Twitter I would read tweets about how hard a time women were having dating. I could not understand what they were finding so difficult until I started reading how and what they thought about dating and men. Let's just say women in general are just not honest about dating and what to expect. For example, one of the biggest trending topics on Twitter a few years ago was $200 dates. Expecting a $200 date is ridiculous, not that $200 dates never happen, but to expect them is ridiculous.

That's not the only ridiculous thing I noticed women talking about on Twitter. When it comes to dating, women in general have a lot of outlandish expectations. But, it's not just the women on Twitter who have outlandish expectations. The number of male "dating gurus" who spout the most sexist dating drivel has somehow skyrocketed in popularity. I am not sure why women like and follow men to learn how to date. These men aren't women. They don't know anything about how to date men.

When these "dating guru" tweets would come across my timeline I had to wonder why they thought they could advise women on how to date. Exactly where did they get their authority? While men may have a pointer here and there for women on dating, until they have actually dated a man, their perspective is limited to what they wish women would do, and often that is something subservient and sexist. Do yourself a favor, ignore the male Twitter "dating gurus." They have no idea what they are talking about. (And, I am sure once they get wind of this book they will be coming for me).

That said, if you are reading this book to find a husband, Stop Now! This book is not for you. I am not writing this book for women who want to get married. Marriage has never been an end goal or a sign of success in dating for me so if that's why you are here you probably should save your money. I am here to talk about dating, that is learning to enjoy another's company, in "more than a friend" type of way. If a relationship or even a marriage comes out of it, that's great, but this book is not going to teach you how to "snag a husband." If that's what you are expecting, then put this book down right now. (Seriously, put it down). If you want to learn something new keep reading.

My goal in this book is to help women end unrealistic expectations in dating and replace them with new realistic ones. I hope to help many women free their minds from sexist dating expectations and sexism in general. I also hope to help women understand that my unconventional approach to dating will allow them to learn about themselves, have a more successful dating life, enjoy the art of dating, and just be happier in general.

Chapter 1: Dating Fallacies

If you are dating you are in a relationship with that person: The "We went out once so now we are together" Fallacy

"We have been dating for two weeks; he's my man. Besides I don't date a guy unless I think we are going to go somewhere. I don't like wasting my time."

Sound familiar? Do you get upset after going out with a guy a few times only to find out you are not the only woman he's dating? Do you believe men should understand that if you are dating you are "together?" Do you think that more than two dates means you are in a relationship? Do you feel that men "lead you on" a lot? I have actually met more than one woman who thought this way. To be honest I always thought it was ridiculous. A few dates is just that, a few dates. Some women even expressed that they felt as if the man "led them on" because they had a few outings together and it did not develop into a relationship. I have even had conversations with women who went out with a guy "as friends" and became upset because they felt "led on."

Whenever I have encountered these types of attitudes I've wondered why the women assumed they were in a relationship? Was it because they went out a few times? Men don't think this way unless you come across one of those unstable possessive men who think that buying dinner means they own you (stay away from those)! I am sure we have all experienced that guy at the club who buys you a drink and then thinks that means he gets to follow you around the club the rest of the night. The "bugaboo" guy. You know exactly how you feel when this guy buys you a drink. That is exactly what you are doing when you think because you went out a few times you are now in a relationship. When you believe that you are in a relationship because of a few dates, you have turned into the "annoying" guy who bought one drink and now thinks you owe him your time. You are now the "bugaboo" if you think going out with a man for a few dinners means he's your boyfriend. Also, you are hurting yourself in the dating world. Just as we can sense the bugaboo lurking at the club, men can sense

that you are a bugaboo aka "needy," and they w
from you.

The truth is dating does not equal a relationship. Dating is simply the art of getting to know someone. A relationship is an actual stated commitment to one another. So if you and the guy you have been dating haven't stated to one another that you are in a relationship, you are not in a relationship. You are just dating and there is nothing wrong with "just dating."

If you get in the habit of thinking dating = boyfriend you end up missing out on one of the greatest things about dating...options. That's the one thing men got right about dating; date more than one person at a time. (More on that in Chapter 4).

MEN ARE ONLY INTERESTED IN ONE THING: THE "ALL MEN ARE DOGS" FALLACY

"Why date when all men want is sex? I'm not interested in sex; I want more, that's why I don't bother dating."

While it is true, men often do try to get women in bed (they are men; what can I say)? However, most men are not **just** interested in sex. Men like companionship just as much as women. In fact, while the stereotype is that women want to be in relationships more than men, and are more likely to want commitment than men, and are more emotional than men, the truth is most men actually like being in a relationship with a woman. Men flourish when they feel they are dating someone they really like and who likes them. In fact, most men, when they are with a woman they really love and are attached to do better in their personal lives and careers. Women make men better. The connection and attachment are more powerful for men than for women; sex is often not the main goal for men in dating. If you don't believe me, think about a man who was dumped by a woman they really liked; it's a sad sight. Occasionally you will find one who just wants sex, but their sexual desires are usually obvious and can be avoided. (More on that in Chapter 5). So no, not all men are dogs. You just need to know what to look for.

And let's be honest, women like sex just as much as men, and are quite capable of carrying on purely sexual relationships. However, to believe that all men want is to have sex with you means you don't think you have much else to offer. If you are afraid to date because you think men only want sex from you, you should really search to see what else you bring to the table. If you are only bringing sex that may be why that's the only thing they want. (More on this in Chapter 6).

IF A MAN DOESN'T TAKE ME ON AN EXPENSIVE DATE HE ISN'T WORTHY OF MY TIME: THE "$200 DATE" FALLACY

"If a man doesn't spend a lot of money on me up front that shows that he's not really worth my time. I deserve to be fawned over and spoiled. No guy should ever take me to a fast food restaurant on a first date; I'm worth more than that."

Sound familiar? If you believe that a man's interest or worthiness is equal to the amount of money he spends on you then you have basically said you are for sale. You are the reason men have created something called "pussy budgets." A "pussy budget" is how much a man will spend in expectation of you having sex with him because you and women like you have decided that your company has a monetary value. I didn't make up the "pussy budget" thing; a guy told me about it. Yes, it's real. Yes, it's stupid, but that's not the point.

Equating your worth to money is indicative of a self-esteem issue. Would you feel worthless if a man spends nothing on you but time? If so, that's sad. You could quite possibly be passing up on someone whose personality is perfectly matched to yours just because you do not realize you have connected your self-esteem to monetary value.

The truth is, how much a man spends on you is not indicative of his interest or love. Men with a lot of money can and sometimes do spend a lot of money on a woman. And chances are he is spending money on more than one woman. Just because a man is spending money on a woman or multiple women doesn't mean he loves them or even has long-term interests in them; he just knows what he's buying.

Before you say that a man can spend money on a woman he loves, yes, that is true. However, money still doesn't equal love. You can buy someone you love a gift but even without the gift you would still love them and they would (hopefully) still love you.

"I don't understand why I'm single. Look at me. Any man would be lucky to date me. I get asked out but I never get asked out on a second date. I don't understand why. I look good."

Does this sound like you or someone you know? I've got news for you. It doesn't matter what you look like. Being pretty is not indicative of a successful dating life. What I have learned about many attractive women who are single is that they don't understand that dating is a skill. Just because you're cute doesn't mean you know how to date. There are a bunch of single pretty women in the world and there are a bunch of very average looking non-single women. Attractive single women could learn a few lessons from these average looking ladies, most of all humility.

If you believe you should have a better time dating because of your looks, you have entitlement issues (and quite possibly some self-esteem issues). A lot of women fall into this category. Physical attractiveness can be an asset, but it is not the end all be all. You need to bring more to the table. No one wants to be in the company of someone who has nothing else to offer except their physical appearance. (More on this in Chapter 4).

"There are no good men. All the good men are taken. If you are over 30, it's too late to find a good man."

This is nonsense. First of all, the "good guy" thing is a fallacy in itself. People are people. Everyone is capable of good or bad behavior. Even a person you love can hurt you. Truth is the so called "good guy" has done way more damage to dating women than the so called "bad" ones. Why? Because women let their guards down to men who appear "good." That's life.

Secondly, you have probably rejected a man who was "good for you." Chances are you have rejected men who are "good for you" multiple times. In fact, there is probably a good chance there are at least three men who are good for you in your life right now that you have overlooked. Often, some of the best for you men are constantly overlooked because either they

14

are just "too nice" or you have "friend zoned" them for whatever reason.

Your definition of "good" is probably a list in your head that you created of completely unrealistic criteria. Since no man can live up to that list, you automatically believe there are no "good" men. Meanwhile, great guys are all around you (and probably some who like you) wondering why you can't see what's right in front of you.

There are plenty of single men out there. Seriously, there are a lot of single men out there. In fact, the men reading this book right now are celebrating for pointing them out. Don't worry, we will talk more about the single men all around you later.

THE "ONE" IS OUT THERE WAITING TO FIND YOU: THE "PRINCESS" FALLACY

You've dreamed of your Prince in shining armor coming into your life and sweeping you off your feet. Your soulmate is out there, just waiting to cross paths with you for your "happily ever after." He's out there somewhere just waiting for you, you know, the "One."

It's unfortunate that this story is sold to women from childhood. Seriously, how many fairytales have this storyline? How sad it is that girls are indoctrinated into this belief from before preschool. Sorry to burst your bubble, but waiting for the "one" guy, the one "true love," the "knight in shining armor," to find you is a fantasy. This princess fairytale has been deeply ingrained in society and in your mind. This is not to say there isn't a person, or several persons, you will deeply connect with. It is possible. That one may be real. But, the idea that there is only ONE man for you in the world is foolishness. There's probably a few thousand.

Truth is there are several men in the world who are compatible with you. You just don't know it yet. Learning how to recognize who you are compatible with is the key. And, no he will not be rescuing you. Ok, well maybe he could, but it is highly unlikely.

MEN DON'T TAKE WOMEN WHO SLEEP AROUND SERIOUSLY: THE "YOU CAN'T TURN A WHORE INTO A HOUSEWIFE" FALLACY

It is on Twitter all the time, men and women "slut shaming" women who basically have put it all out there sexually. These women have claimed their sexuality and projected it out for the world to see. This opens them up to the criticism of, how could any woman be so "loose?" She will never be wholesome; no man will ever want her, because no man "wifes" up "hoes".... Let me inform you, contrary to popular belief women who have slept around do get married, all the time, in fact. As Jamilah Lemieux has provocatively pointed out on Twitter, "Hoes don't exist." In fact, the way I see it, women who have slept around get "wifed up" more frequently than women who haven't. Let's take one famous example of a woman who we have all known to have had sex, Kim Kardashian. She has a sex tape. She is known for her "assets." She is also known to have been the girlfriend of more than one famous man. Basically, to the world she's "been around." But, guess what? She's married.

It is sexism that dictates that a woman's value is diminished by having multiple sexual partners, whether true or perceived. It is a fallacy created as a way to control the sexual behavior of women. The sad part is women project this fallacy onto themselves. This is a divide and conquer technique that makes one group of women think they are better because they are "chaste." In reality, people date, fall in love, and get married with all sorts of sexual history.

The judgmental sexist men reading this may be thinking to themselves that women can't date like men. Although most of them have multiple sexual partners, from their viewpoint these women will still be "hoes" and no one will want to date them. I would just like to tell these sexist boys to…"Shut up." Even the women you call "hoes" don't want you. Stop judging and slut shaming women and go try to figure out why women don't like you.

THERE IS SOMETHING SERIOUSLY WRONG WITH EVERY GUY I DATE: THE "IT'S NOT ME, IT'S THEM" FALLACY

You date, in fact you date pretty often. You have been out with every type of guy, even guys who aren't "your type." You've done the work; you are in the trenches. And every single man you've been out with has something wrong with him, in your opinion. He's too cocky; he's not ambitious enough; he eats with his hands... But, please notice something. The only common factor between you and all the men you date is you. It is a mathematical impossibility for every single man you date to have something wrong with him. The common denominator is you and the truth is, if you find something wrong with EVERY man you date, chances are very good there is something wrong with **you**.

CHAPTER 2: MANAGING EXPECTATIONS

"The man I want to date has to be
   -6' 5"
   -drive a luxury car
   -have no children
   -come from a two parent home
   -be a corporate executive
   -have an amazing body
   -have a retirement fund
   -know how to golf
   -like movies
   -love dogs
   -..."

Does this remind you of you? You've planned out exactly what you want in a man. You have listed all of your requirements. You may have even posted these

21

.ns on your vision boards because you know he's out there. So far you have turned down every single man who's asked you out because he has not met your listed requirements at face value. I am all for writing down goals and envisioning what you want for your future, however, writing down a list of requirements for another person isn't realistic. If you have a list of requirements that a man has to meet to date you, you should probably go ahead and toss that list into the garbage. Yep, throw it away. Toss it out. Forget you even made this list of requirements. Why? Because the chances of you meeting a man who meets your requirements is extremely rare, if not impossible. In fact, if you did meet a man who met these requirements, he probably would not date you.

Please do not take me telling you to throw away your list as me being mean. I am being realistic and honest and am probably the only person who will say this to you. Know this, I am not trying to be hurtful, to kill your dreams, or saying that men who meet your list of requirements don't exist. They actually do. Yes, men who have all the requirements on your list do actually exist, somewhere. Let me reiterate, those men who meet the exact requirements of your list do actually exist; they are not unicorns or fantasies. The problem is your chances of meeting them are very rare, and if you

did happen to meet one, he more than likely wc
not date you.

Chances are if you are fantasizing about a man
with all the requirements on your list, you do not know
any men like that. This means you are not in a league
where men like this exist. (More on leagues later in
Chapter 4). This also means that if you did come across
one of these men, he probably would not date you. Of
course, you don't have to take my word for it. Just tell
me how many men who meet your list of
requirements, you've met and have also asked you out
on a date? I'll wait…

Stop looking for a fairytale

There are other women who do not have a list
but they have an exact fantasy of what they expect
dating a man to be like.

> "The man I date will take me to
> my favorite restaurant on our first
> date. He will fall in love with me
> right away. He will take me to
> meet his parents after we date for

three weeks. He will propose to me with a five carat diamond ring with a princess setting after we have dated for three months. We will have a destination wedding with fifty guests. Two years after we are married we will have our first baby..."

Does this remind you of you? You know exactly who you want and how he is going to come to you. You have planned the perfect relationship in your mind and you won't "settle" for anything less. Why should you settle? You are worth what you desire, in fact you deserve no less, right?

Fairytales. Recognize them, enjoy them in your imagination, maybe even write them in a novel, then come back to reality. They aren't happening, and if they do it's **rare**. Again, I am not being mean, just realistic and honest. Your fantasy of dating is just that, a fantasy. Enjoy it, then come on back to reality because your fantasy is not real. Dating requires you to operate in the real world, not in a fantasy.

Many women are often discouraged with their dating lives because their expectations are rooted in fantasy. They are deeply disappointed by their real dating experiences because they are nothing like their fantasies. A woman can even meet someone who fits her list or her fantasy, but then quickly find out that the man isn't compatible and the fantasy is ruined. There are also those situations where couples rush to get married because the fantasy fits even though there are red flags everywhere. Yet, because they don't want to give up the fantasy they go through with getting married anyway. (The weddings are gorgeous though)! These fantasy marriages often end up divorced within a few months because reality finally shows up, leading to further disappointment.

It is very important when dating to effectively manage your expectations. If you have a list of requirements or a fairytale in your mind and your date doesn't match your fantasy/list you are going to be greatly disappointed. In fact, I've noticed many women talking about how disappointed they are when they date. I already know it is because the men they have dated did not meet their expectations. Why? Most likely because their expectations were unrealistic.

You must be realistic about dating. You must be realistic about your expectations. When you have sensible expectations, or rather no expectations at all, you are unlikely to be disappointed.

Unrealistic expectations are rooted in a sense of entitlement. Women in our society have gotten to a point where they believe that they are entitled to the man they think they want. (Don't worry ladies, men have also gotten to a point where they feel entitled to unrealistic expectations too, just in a different way). I don't know what causes this entitlement, maybe it's the movies we watch, maybe it's the books we read, but we have definitely gotten to a point in our society where women feel genuinely entitled to have exactly what they want in a man, without once looking at what they need or what they bring to the table. This sense of entitlement is creating unrealistic expectations in dating and even greater disappointment.

WHAT SHOULD YOU ACTUALLY EXPECT?

Women have been taught a fantasy about dating since childhood. Girls are told they are all princesses and some day a prince will show up. He will be perfect and love her forever. (Or he will be less th perfect but the girl will forgive his imperfections because he is handsome or rich)! A lot of women think they are immune to this fantasy but trust me, this fantasy is planted subconsciously in the minds of women over and over from childhood to adulthood to the point where women have this expectation of dating the "perfect guy." Well, to burst your fantasy bubble, there are no perfect men. They don't exist. (Even Idris Elba isn't perfect. He's close though…). Seriously, this fantasy just isn't real. Prince Charming isn't coming. You won't be swept off your feet. There is no happily ever after.

Have I popped your fantasy bubble? Good. I want you to let go of all your fantasies. I want you to start approaching dating with a clean slate, with no preconceived notions or ideas. I want you to learn how to date from a totally new perspective, to have realistic expectations. I want you to know what you should actually expect while dating. And what should you expect when dating? **Nothing**. That's right, nothing except meeting up with someone new. That means you just meet up with a new guy and get to know him. You don't expect anything more. It's just a moment in time with a guy you want to get to know. Nothing else. This might seem difficult to you right now. It's not, but giving up your expectations is a difficult thing to do in the beginning because you want to expect something, a doctor, a lawyer, a type of restaurant, a type of car, something. However, expecting nothing is exactly what you should expect. Nothing at all except meeting up with someone new.

Women who have the hardest time in the dating world are those who refuse to give up their fantasies about dating. You may be rolling your eyes and fighting with me in your head right now for telling you to expect nothing. Women like you don't want to give up on the idea of Prince Charming. I promise you though, if you let these fantasies go, these fantastic "ideas" about dating, you will open yourself up to greater possibilities of dating, relationships, and love, that you didn't even know existed. Dating will become enjoyable and stimulating instead of disappointing and burdensome. You will begin to learn to expect the unexpected, and you will end up loving to date.

On your next date you must mentally prepare yourself to expect only to spend time with a man you want to get to know. You should not expect him to show up in a certain type of vehicle. You should not expect a meal. You should not expect him to take you to a certain level of restaurant. You should not expect a gift. You should not expect him to spend a certain amount of money for the evening. You should not expect anything except spending time with a guy you want to get to know. That's it. If you are disappointed with that, then you expect too much out of dating.

What about physical aesthetics?

"I only want to date a guy who
is this tall, weighs this much, is
this size, is this color, has this
color eyes..."

Yes, we all have physical preferences to which we are attracted and we all want to attract the absolutely most handsome man ever. But, let's be real about expectations. Most men are average, average height, average weight, average appearance. If you are limiting yourself to men who only fit certain physical characteristics you are setting yourself up for unrealistic expectations. I am not saying you have to date an ugly guy, or that you have to settle. I am saying that the guy who is only 5'8" may become a lot cuter once you get to know him. When you find yourself attracted to someone, especially because of who they are on the inside, the outside will automatically become more appealing. It is equally true that a person who may appear outwardly attractive can quickly become unattractive if they are nasty personality wise. Remember, there is beauty in everyone. So stop placing physical limits on who you will go out with. You could be eliminating men from your dating pool who are most compatible with you. Men who may be exactly what you want. Men you eliminated because you decided that they did not fit your physical expectations.

WHAT YOU SHOULD BE LOOKING FOR

Compatibility. Compatibility is ultimately what everyone wants and needs in a partner. When you date you want to "click" with someone, feel some connection, have some similar interests, do things you both find fun. Forget that opposites attract nonsense. Sure they may attract, but eventually they will repel the hell out of each other, especially in closed quarters. So look for someone who makes you feel comfortable, that you have a lot in common with, whose company you truly enjoy. That's what you are looking for when you date. You want to find out how compatible you are with the person sitting across from you. The more you find in common the more time you will want to spend with that person.

SHOULD YOU STILL GO FOR WHAT YOU WANT?

I have made you throw away your list; I have killed your fantasy. I have told you that most men are physically average, and have told you that what you really want is compatibility. So now you are wondering, "Do I get to date the guy I want?" The answer is "yes," you do get to date the guy you want.

But right now, you don't know what you want. That's right, you don't know what you want. You think you do. That's why you had a list right? The truth is most people have no idea what they want when they date, they only know what they fantasize about. In order to find out what you truly want you have to figure it out. The way you figure it out is learning about yourself. You do this by spending time with different types of people. By taking the time to learn about others you will also learn about yourself. Dating will help you learn how to identify what you really like about yourself and about men. It will also help you know what you dislike. You will learn about yourself and what you truly desire from a man. This book will help guide you through your dating experiences to help you understand how to attract exactly what you want once you learn what that is.

Chapter 3: Being Honest About Yourself

It's time to ask yourself, "What image do I present to men?"

Answer these questions AND BE HONEST!

- *What image do you present to men? e.g. Are you smart, funny, sexy, friendly, geeky?*
- *What does your image say about you? e.g. Independent, career woman, nurturing?*
- *Are you confident or unsure?*
- *Happy or miserable?*
- *Approachable or unapproachable?*
- *What **exactly** does your image say to men?*
- *How do you know what you think your image is saying is true?*

Often women are delusional about what their image says about them. (Men, do not get excited about this statement. You often are delusional about yourselves too). Women often are dishonest with themselves about everything from their personalities to their physical features. I have already talked about being realistic about your expectations. It is now time to be realistic about yourself. You say you are a "good woman" who deserves a "good man," but when you are placed in front of an "honesty mirror" does your image really say "broken, tired, lonely, and desperate?" The truth is if you were as "good" as you say you are, dating would not be difficult for you. There is a reason you are not dating the way you would like to. Not only are your expectations unrealistic, the image you present to the world is not attractive.

Being attractive is not just a physical thing. I repeat, being attractive is not just a physical thing. Attractiveness has to do with everything about you from your personality, your attitude, your outlook on life, to your physical features. Please understand, believing that only certain physical traits attract men is a fallacy. No matter what you look like, some man somewhere will find you attractive (as long as you are exuding the best you of course). I am sure many of you are thinking, "But only women who look like _____ attract men." First of all, you must never compare yourself to anyone else. You are a beautiful, unique individual who is attractive. Before you start to believe that only women who look a certain way or have certain physical traits have an easier time dating than you do, remember women of all sizes, ages, races... have just as much difficulty dating (and are probably reading this book right now). The truth is, men love women, period. There is not one physical "type" of woman who is more successful at dating than another physical type. Men love women of all races, heights, sizes... There is not one type of eye color, hair color, hair type... that is more successful at dating than another. Sure each individual man may have preferences, but so do you. The point is to always know you are beautiful as you are. Men are attracted to you as you are.

If you believe you have to resort to drastically changing yourself to attract men you may be dealing with some self-esteem issues. The truth is, no matter what you look like some man somewhere thinks you are the most attractive woman in the world. Never compare yourself to other women and be confident in who you are. Confidence makes you more attractive. There is only one you, so be you. Men will like you as you are. However, if the image you project to the world is unattractive, meaning that you send out negative/unattractive energy in some way, men will not be attracted to you and will not want to date you.

I am reminded of the "Sex and the City" episode where Carrie is dating Berger and all of Carrie's girlfriends finally get to hang out with Berger. Miranda talks about her most recent date and wonders if her date will ever call. Berger interjects with "He's just not that into you,"[1] an honest, yet shocking revelation to which all of the other women protest that Berger doesn't know what he's talking about. Miranda, however, finds his honesty refreshing. She no longer has to guess what's going on with the man she went out with. This is the type of honesty you must have when you assess your image. You must figure out why "He's just not that into you." If you cannot be this honest with yourself I recommend getting an "honesty mirror."

What is an "honesty mirror" you may ask. An "honesty mirror" is a man, a friend, a cousin, a coworker, that you trust to be honest with you. My "honesty mirror" is my older brother, Tarik. I know that whatever I ask him, he will be completely honest with

---

[1] "Pick-A-Little, Talk-A-Little." *Sex and the City.* HBO. July 13, 2003. Television.

me from a male perspective. Once you find you_ "honesty mirror" ask him what it is about you that men may not find attractive. Note: your "honesty mirror" **cannot** be a man who may potentially want to date you! A guy who wants to date you is going to tell you what you want to hear and not be an "honesty mirror."

When you find your "honesty mirror" tell him you want his honest opinion. Tell him to go in, not hold back, and rip off the bandaid. Then put on your thick skin and be prepared. Men often can be brutally honest, but trust me, you want the truth. Plus, honesty is refreshing even when it hurts. It is important that we surround ourselves with people who will be honest with us. Honest people can and do save us from a lot of heartache and pain in life. Hurt feelings go away a lot faster than depression. Do not be afraid of someone being honest with you. Remember "iron sharpens iron," so if your "honesty mirror" 'goes there' with you, thank him.

Asking your girlfriends to be your "honesty mirror" in general will not help. Women are a lot more empathetic than men and are more likely to tell you what you want to hear, being compelled to spare your feelings. You can sometimes find a female friend who will not spare your feelings but in general female friends will not tell you, if they actually know what unattractive traits you are projecting. I believe this is because women also tend to want to save their friends' self-esteem. Plus, your female friends are not dating you and most likely will not be able to see the negative traits men who are interested in dating you see.

Men in general are usually not as merciful as women when it comes to judgment. You will need to mentally prepare yourself when you talk to your "honesty mirror." You may really get your feelings hurt. However, it is better to know the truth about what negative traits you are projecting. If you do not know you will not be able to change them. While you may get upset at your "honesty mirror" you will come to appreciate them in the long run since knowing the truth about yourself is always helpful.

After you have had your chance to look into your "honesty mirror" and know what unattractive traits you have been projecting, it is time to change them.

The most frequent unattractive traits men complain about are:

- bad attitude
- bad manners

- bad hygiene
- low self-esteem

Changing unattractive traits is crucial if you truly desire to have a happy dating experience. Exhibiting unattractive traits will make negative dating experiences continually happen to you.

BAD ATTITUDE

Many of my male friends have complained about dating women with bad attitudes. (Again men, don't get excited, I have had female friends complain about men with bad attitudes as well). They have shared multiple stories of women who complain through the whole date or who were simply just rude. It bothers me to think that a person would take the time to go out with someone only to taint the experience with negativity. Honestly, what's the point? No one wants to be around a person who constantly complains or is constantly unhappy or that makes them feel bad. I completely understand why these women are having a hard time dating. No one wants to be around them. If you are a woman who generally has a bad attitude, now is the time to consciously change it to a positive one. Simply changing your attitude could completely change your dating experiences.

If any part of this rings true, diligently search yourself to understand why you put out so much negativity. Is it something you learned? Were the adults in your life constantly complaining when you were a child? Many times we pick up habits we learned from our parents. Very often we do not even notice these habits or know where they came from. Generally speaking, if your mom or dad complained constantly as you were growing up, chances are you will too. Yes, attitudes can be learned and passed down from one generation to the next. Changing your attitude happens when you become self-aware. Self-awareness is crucial to having a positive dating life. Once you are aware of your attitude then you can consciously begin to change it. When you are not self-aware you may not even notice your attitude. For example, if you complain a lot, by becoming self-aware, you can consciously start to not complain. Attitude has a lot to do with self-awareness and self-assessment. Make every effort to constantly check yourself. This ensures that you are sending out positivity instead of negativity.

Male friends have also told me stories of women having bad manners on dates. Ok, I must admit I find it hard to believe, but apparently there are still some out there who chew with their mouths open, wipe their faces with their sleeves, or even sneeze without covering their mouths. There are even some who simply do not use the basics of saying please and thank you. In fact, men very often complain that women do not say thank you. It matters. Please make sure you always thank your date afterwards; it is very important.

It is actually scary to think that there are adults who still do not have manners. However, if you do have bad manners, now is the time to be polite. Perhaps you simply were never taught proper etiquette. That's ok. Just make sure you take time to learn. Pick up a book on etiquette. You could be sending out a negative image simply because you are not doing the smallest thing by just being polite.

BAD HYGIENE

If you have bad hygiene (bad dental hygiene is one of the greatest complaints) now is the time to fix it. If you practice regular basic hygiene and still have issues this may be indicative of a health issue so please see a physician or dentist. I had a guy tell me of his dating experience with a woman who had bad breath. He said she was absolutely beautiful but had a bad case of halitosis. He actually told her that she had an issue and should see a dentist. She did and fixed the issue. She also thanked him later.

I know often we want to err on the side of being polite by not telling people about hygiene issues so that we do not embarrass them. However, if people were more honest (and also more open to honesty) we could all help one another. So, if your "honesty mirror" points out a hygiene or health issue, thank them.

LOW SELF-ESTEEM

If you have low self-esteem, you really need to focus on yourself instead of dating. Having low self-esteem attracts abusive personality types. Being in an abusive relationship will only make your self-esteem worse. You must first repair any self-esteem issues before you start dating. Low self-esteem is like a homing beacon to asshole and douchebag types of men. They also have low self-esteem and in turn will make you feel bad to make themselves feel better. I highly recommend that if you are dealing with low self-esteem that you seek help from a professional counselor. Counseling is very helpful. Once you work through your self-esteem issues you will be much happier and in a much better position to date. **The truth is you will never be happy dating if you are not already happy with yourself.**

Who do you attract?

Be honest. What type of man approaches you the most? Is he polite? Smart? Does he seem confident? Is he respectful in his approach? Or, is he rude and cocky? The concept of we are who we attract is very real. If you are constantly approached by men who you do not consider worthy of your attention then you need to figure out what signals you are sending out that makes these types of men attracted to you. Yes, you are attracting the men that you think you don't want. Something about you makes them want to approach you. It can be anything from how you look, to what you are wearing, to how you carry yourself. We all get a couple of street hecklers every now and then, but I am talking about the men who normally ask you out. If these men are not the men you would like to ask you out, then you are sending out something that is attracting them and therefore you need to figure out what that is. But, on the flip side…

WHO DO YOU REJECT?

Are you positive the type of men you say you want are not approaching you? A lot of women say they want to date "successful" men, but how are you judging what success is when a man approaches you? Many women look to material things as a measure of success. They are looking at how a man dresses or what kind of car he drives, just material things. If you are one of those women who do that, stop. Sure material things are nice. We all like nice things, but there are plenty of people with nice things and no "success" and plenty of people with "success" who don't care much for a lot of material things. It is impossible to tell who someone is from just one look. That is why you must take the time to get to know the men whom you will date.

When you immediately reject a man without taking the time to really get to know him you could be missing out on what you really want. Usually women reject men based on looks or some other surface reason. *You must stop doing that.* Just because a guy isn't 6 feet or driving the type of car you prefer does not mean he isn't worth getting to know. He could very well be that "successful" guy you were looking for, even in his t-shirt and jeans. You have to stop looking at just the "cover" of the book and start reading it.

Chapter 4: Learning How to Date

HOW SHOULD A MAN ASK YOU OUT?

What you want to notice when a man approaches you is not his car, not his clothes, not his jewelry, but how he treats you. Only how he treats you. You are looking for a man to ask you out **respectfully, engagingly, and with genuine interest.** That's it. Not a car, not a suit, not a watch. **Respect, engagement, and interest.**

When a man approaches you with these three attributes it says three very important things:

• He respects you. Respect is very important. You do not want to date a person who will turn around and be a jerk to you when he doesn't get what he wants. Most men who will eventually be disrespectful to u, are disrespectful from the moment you meet them. Think about it.

- He took the time to engage you. Men see women whom they find attractive all the time, however, getting the woman to actually pay enough attention to them to ask them out is not easy. If a man gets your attention long enough for you to consider a date, that's a big deal. Imagine if you had to ask men out. How would you engage their attention? It is not as easy as it looks. So make sure you acknowledge the effort.

- He is genuinely interested. You do not want to date someone who is only asking you out to be a backup plan for something else. Genuine interest is necessary for the date to turn out well. If he is not genuinely interested in going out with you, pass. He is not worth the time.

SHOULD YOU ASK A MAN OUT?

Honestly, everyone is different. I don't ask men out because I know that men go after what they want. (More on that in Chapter 5). Plus, if you ask a man out, you can't tell if he is genuinely interested. He may but usually when a man asks you out, you can better gauge his interest and not waste time with a person who isn't seriously interested in you. I know this sounds sexist but, social conditioning has a lot to do with dating. While I will never knock a woman for asking a man out if she wants to, I also understand that men who take the time to ask a woman out really do want to go out with her. Knowing that you are going out with a man who definitely wants to be out with you is definitely going to make the experience better.

SHOULD HE CALL YOU OR TEXT YOU TO ASK YOU OUT?

This is one of the "great debates" amongst my girlfriends. Is it wrong for a guy to ask you out by text? The truth is, it doesn't matter. As long as a guy respectfully engaged you in person to ask for your number, it is perfectly fine for him to ask you out by text or by call. Why? Because as long as he approached you in person and asked for your number he still showed the signs of genuine interest. Also, texting is a normal part of our social communication now. If you are a stickler for not dating men who do not call you to ask you out you will limit yourself based on a very arbitrary rule. You may also miss out on a very fun date.

DATE MORE THAN ONE MAN AT A TIME

Dating is a numbers game for women too. Just because you went out with a guy does not mean you are not free to go out with another. It's important to understand that when you are "dating," you should be doing exactly that, **dating**. That means feel free to accept as many dates as your calendar can hold. I once accepted three dates in one day. (It was a great day by the way)! Some of you are probably freaking out by me telling you this, but trust me, dating more than one person is the key to learning how to date. It is also the key to figuring out what you really want. (More on why you should date more than one man in "If a man asks you out respectfully, say yes" section of this chapter).

Yes, there are leagues in dating. Before you roast me, hear me out. It is probably better to call leagues "circles" since saying "league" sometimes leads one to believe someone's social status is elevated above someone else's. This is not true and this is not what I mean. I mean, "Water seeks its own level." In general, people from certain backgrounds, education level, income level, social life style, only date other people from similar backgrounds. Even race is a circle. In general, a person who is wealthy does not date a person who is not wealthy. This is not to say it doesn't happen but when it does happen it is rare. Why? Because people stay within their own circles. This is why interracial dating, while more common now than ever, is still in general slightly controversial because people who date someone of a different race are stepping outside of their normal circle.

Normally, if you are in one circle the chances of you crossing paths with someone from a different circle on a social level does not happen frequently. While it is certainly possible to jump out of your circle into another, it is highly improbable. It can be done but it takes effort, often effort most people are unwilling to give because they are already comfortable in their circle. This is often why people have "preferences" when it comes to the race of the person they date. They are comfortable with what they are familiar with. Dating someone of a different race often requires one to move beyond their own social circle.

And now, time for more honesty. Most women believe that no man is out of their league (aka circle)! I am here to tell you that is not true. There are men who are out of your league (circle)! That's a fact. The men who are out of your league are out of it because you will never have the opportunity to be in their circles to meet them or you just do not have the "resume" so to speak, that will make them want to ask you out. Here I am killing your fantasy again... sure you'd like to date the famous actor but honestly where are you going to have the opportunity to meet him and get to know him to the point where he will actually ask you out? It's time to be realistic again… the actor, the musician, the CEO, the lawyer, the doctor...unless you are already in those circles, he is out of your league. It happens, accept it and move on.

You need to ask yourself who is in your league. Look around you. What do you do? Where do you hang out? Who are your friends? What circles are you in? Who are the men in your circles? Have you dated any of them? Or, have you just completely ignored the men who are already around you? I've noticed that many women have ignored the men right around them in hopes of dating someone they perceive as a better option whether real or imagined, when it could be quite possible to find a great person to date right "in their own backyard" so to speak. Do not discount the men who are right around you. There are many wonderful single men who are often overlooked because they are right in your own circle. Many times these men are the most compatible men for you because you already share many of the same interests because you already share a circle. Also, staying in your own league can be a fun and rewarding experience so don't be so quick to dismiss the men you already know and interact with. A man who is "good for you" could be right up under your nose.

I believe the biggest problem with saying the word "league" is that there is a perception of leagues being higher or lower; this is not true. However, for lack of a better description, when you are dating "out of your league," you may find it extremely challenging because you will have to put in extra effort to move into a different social circle. It is extremely difficult to jump into a new social circle. People who are already in the circle will eye you with suspicion. You may not even be welcome in some circles. Humans are tribal. There is no way around it. Even a person who appears to be an "outsider" to most people, has a circle they are most comfortable with. And, even if you end up dating someone "out of your league" for lack of a better description, you may find yourself suddenly uncomfortable and unable to deal with the pressure of being in a new circle.

What about dating someone whom you or your friends would consider "out of his league?" The problem you run into there is as similar as dating someone "out of your league." It's challenging because the man who wants to date you will be eyed with suspicion from your peers and possibly even you. And, if he isn't completely secure with himself, your relationship with him could lead to problems down the line. He may not be able to deal with the expectations and pressures of your "circle." (Think about when a "white collar" woman dates a "blue collar" man). I am not saying that it won't work, but be prepared for the challenges. You could be quite happy with someone who is not in "your league," but if you both do not have an understanding of your relationship you both could crack under societal circle pressures. This is often why you do not see celebrities dating noncelebrity or non-industry people. It's just easier. It doesn't mean it does not happen, but for the most part it is just easier to relate to someone similar to you.

WHAT DO YOU REALLY WANT TO FEEL WHEN YOU GO ON A DATE?

Connected. You want to date someone who you find a connection with. How do you connect with someone? You take time to get to know them. You talk. You share. I cannot stress enough that compatibility is gravely important when dating someone. The more you have in common, the more you have to talk about, the more you can connect to one another, the more fun you will have. How do you get to feel this way? You have to take the time to get to know a person. **Dating is a skill** and it takes practice.

STOP HUSBAND SHOPPING

If you are reading this book because you want a husband just stop reading now. This book isn't about getting married; it's about dating. I've encountered more than one woman in my lifetime who would not date a man because she couldn't see him as a potential husband, which some think is the best way to go. Some women only date a guy if she thinks the date will lead to marriage or a serious relationship. If you are one of these women who is searching for a husband, you are not dating, you are shopping. You are looking for a guy who fits some requirements you have created in your mind, a fantasy. Stop doing that. If you want to date you need to understand the reality. Dating is taking time to get to know someone. That's it. You give your time and in turn a man gives his time to you so that you both get to know each other.

While I understand why people do this, they have a goal in mind and don't want to waste time with someone they do not see as a potential mate. However, they often skip over people because of surface reasons which should never be used to determine someone's potential long-term compatibility. In reality, most people do not know what they are looking for in a potential partner. People have a fantasy of what they want for a partner, but not a realistic idea.

Before your next date you should get rid of your preconceived notions of whom your date should be. Dating is not you interviewing a man for your husband job. You are not a hiring manager looking to fill a new husband position. You do not get to pick out the model of husband you want on the first date. A man is not a car, although I know we sometimes wish that they were. (At least then we would know exactly what we are getting up front). When dating, you and your date are on equal footing, you get to know him and he gets to know you. That's it. In some ways women do have the upper hand because we usually have way more choices in terms of whom we date. However, when dating, we are just getting to know the other person. So allow yourself to meet someone new and get to know him. Do not look for a future, just enjoy the moment together. You never know what can come out of a date. You may not make a love connection but you may find a new business contact, a new friend, or maybe even find one of your friends a great guy. What you need to make sure you are not doing is automatically dismissing your opportunity to get to know a guy because he doesn't fit your image for your future.

DATING SHOULD BE FUN

If your dating experience up to this point has been miserable, you've been dating all wrong. Dating should always be fun. If your dates have not been fun then it is time to change your approach. I have never had a bad date, ever, and I have been on plenty. In fact, the times in my life when I have been single I've always looked forward to dating because for me dating is truly a lot of fun. Even on those dates where I knew we would never be a couple, I still had a great time. Even when the dates got a little awkward or weird, it was still fun. No matter what, when you date the main point is to have fun. In order to have fun you have to have absolutely **no expectations**.

Just go with the flow. If he asks you to meet him in the park for a stroll and a hot dog from the hot dog stand…Go. (If you don't eat meat, still go, have a pretzel). If he asks you to check out a concert of an artist you have never heard of…Go. If he asks you to go see a movie you would never choose to see…Go. What do you have to lose? Nothing. Nothing is lost in a new experience. Even if you don't become a fan of the artist or movie he chose, you have gained a new experience. The point is to just enjoy the company. It's really that simple.

But, what about the "Netflix and chill" phenomenon? I know recently there has been an epidemic of men asking women to go on "dates" at their homes. Personally, I don't find chilling at home to really fall under the definition of "date." I think it is a little too personal to invite someone to your house the first 1-3 times you date. Once you get to know someone, hanging at home may happen. However, until you really get a chance to know a guy, if he asks you to "come over" that is not asking you "out" that's asking you "in." Feel free to decline those.

Now, you are probably wondering, "How exactly do I have fun on every date?" That just seems highly unlikely, and nearly impossible. It's not. However, if you are a negative thinker, you will have a negative experience. In order to always have fun on dates you have to think you are going to have fun. Seriously, you have to think, "This is going to be fun!" You have to expect great things to happen. You have to believe that everything is going to be fun. Basically, you have to change your thinking to only expect positive things on your date. Your positive thinking and your positive attitude will be reciprocated by your date. If your date sees you are happy then amazingly he will feel less pressure and feel happy too. The next thing you know two positive people will be having a great time together. Your thoughts about your date will shape its outcome. If you believe that you are going to have a bad time, I promise you that you will.

Right now many women expect things more than fun on a date, such as a certain type of restaurant or they expect a man to spend a certain amount of money on a date. I have been on dates that cost less than $20 to dates that cost well over $1000 and I had fun on all of them. The amount of money a man spends does not make the experience more or less fun. Sure, dining in Napa is fun, but so is hot chocolate in the middle of the city. The point is, stop putting a monetary value on your time. A man who wants to date you is not paying for your time, he is simply trying to get to know you. Do not ignore a guy who wants to spend time with you because he chooses not to spend an extraordinary amount of money.

Back to positive thinking, I cannot emphasize enough how important a positive attitude and outlook are for your date. These are so important that if you feel that you cannot be positive, you should postpone your date until you do. There really is no point in going on a date if you are going to be negative. You will have a bad time and so will your date. Humans pick up on each other's emotions. That is why it is important to choose to be around positive people. Also, choose to have a positive attitude around others. If you show up for a date and you are already in a foul mood you are more likely to be disappointed in the experience and, of course, put your date in a bad mood as well. No one wants to be responsible for someone else having a bad time. Usually when there is a bad date, the blame falls on the man. So do both of you a favor, if you are having a hard time getting to a positive mental space before your date, just postpone. Both you and your date will be grateful.

BE OPEN

I have heard men tell horror stories of women refusing to eat at certain restaurants or expecting expensive dates and always wondered who these women were and how they became so presumptuous, entitled, and arrogant. Do you really feel that you are too good to eat at a certain place? Do you feel that you are so special that you deserve a man who spends a certain monetary amount on a date? If so, why? Why do you feel this way? This is where self-assessment is so important. If you feel that you should only be taken on expensive dates, you need to assess what insecurities are deep down inside of you that make you feel this way.

Insecurities that lead to entitlement issues mean you probably should not be dating. You should probably take the time to work on yourself instead. The truth is, if someone asks you out, they are offering something to you for nothing but your company. The correct thing to do is be grateful. Now, before you men get crazy and try to take women on a sewer tour or something insane, as long as a man is respectful, it doesn't matter how much the date costs. The point is to get to know him. So, don't worry about how much the date is, just enjoy yourself.

To have a great dating life you have to have no expectations. Seriously, **no expectations**. You have to open yourself up to all of the possibilities that can happen. You have to look for a positive experience in just experiencing a new person. If a man takes you to a "cheap" restaurant for dinner do not take that as an insult to you. The restaurant he chooses for the date is not a reflection of you. It could be possible that the cheap restaurant is all he can afford at the time or maybe, just maybe, that cheap restaurant has the best desserts in the city and he wanted to share that with you. You have no idea why he is taking you there and you won't know unless you go. Just be open. Remember, no expectations.

Often you may find that some of your most memorable dates are when the guy you went out with wasn't trying to "impress" you, but actually get to know you. Sure it's nice to be wined and dined, but really what is the point of a date? To get to know someone better. Allow yourself to not think about where you are going and what you are going to be doing and how much it's costing him, but think about who you are getting to know. Take the date as an opportunity to exchange information about each other. Where you are and what you are doing should not be taken as a major factor, just an ancillary one.

Again for emphasis, **you must get rid of your preconceived images of what you think is supposed to happen on your date**. Allow yourself to be open. One of the reasons I love dating so much is because I have always enjoyed being exposed to new things, whether a new restaurant, a new lounge, or a new gallery, it is the experience. Being open gives you the opportunity to fully enjoy experiencing and learning something new. The more you know and the more you are exposed to, the more interesting you become. Just so you know, men like interesting women. Interesting women are "charming."

Even if you think he isn't attractive, short, or not your "type" if a guy respectfully asks you out, accept it. Remember what I said earlier. What you are looking for when a man approaches you is for him to approach you respectfully, engagingly, and with genuine interest. I never said anything about physical attributes. Respectfully, engagingly, and with genuine interest. Now hear me out; why am I saying accept the date? Several reasons. You think you know what you want in a guy, but honestly you don't (and this is exactly why you are reading this book). What you think you want is what you have created in your imagination out of what you've seen in movies or on TV, what you've read in books, or what you think you know about your friends' relationships. What is in your imagination does not exist. It is not until you have dated several men will you ever know what you really want because only then will you know what is really out there. So, it is time to learn what kind of men really do exist and dating several guys is how you learn. It is also how you learn what you truly want. For now, you should date people you probably would have never given a chance before. But, just bear with me on this. You *need* the experience.

The reason you should accept dates from men who are respectful, engaging, and with genuine interest despite them not being what you think is "your type," is that you do not know how to date. If you did know how to date you wouldn't be seeking dating help. Basically, accepting dates with guys you don't really think you would like is practice for you. **Dating is a skill,** a skill most people are not naturals at. Getting to know someone, learning the art of conversation, and flirting, requires practice to master. Sure some people are naturals at it, but most people aren't. Accepting multiple dates gives you multiple opportunities for practice. Practice really does make perfect. The more you practice, the better you will be at dating. Think about it, what if you do end up on a date with a guy you *really really* like and you haven't had any dating practice. Do you really want to ruin it because you don't know how to get past the uncomfortable silence? Or, what if you are terrible at flirting, is this the guy you want to practice your awkward flirting with? Trust me, you don't. You want your dates to go smoothly. In order to make sure your dates go smoothly you need to practice your dating skills. Practice so much that you become an expert dater. Expert daters are almost certain to get asked on a second date. When you are an expert dater you become such a great date that second and third dates are guaranteed. Until you reach this level you should accept any date that gives you the opportunity to practice your skills.

Not only does dating help you hone your dating skills, dating brings confidence. When you go on multiple dates you will become more comfortable with the idea of getting to know someone new. The idea of meeting up with someone you do not know well will cause less anxiety over time and you will be more at ease. This will allow you to open up more. When it comes down to it the more dates you go on the more confident you will be when it comes to dating because essentially every date you go on is practice. You will begin to know what your strengths are, what your weaknesses are, what works for you, and what doesn't work for you. You won't feel so unsure of yourself when you go out. You will begin to exude confidence. Confidence makes you more attractive. Confident people are more attractive in general. Women are attracted to confident men, and in turn men are attracted to confident women. The more dates you go on, the more confident you will be about going on a date. You will also become more confident in general, which will attract more men to you. More men, more dates.

Dating helps you learn about yourself. Putting yourself in new situations means you will be faced with new experiences. New experiences means new responses. Dating several men will not only help you learn about what you really like in men, you will also learn things about yourself. Suddenly you will start to figure out what you truly find attractive in a man. You will also find out what you do not like. Little quirks will start to show themselves. Once on a date I found out that how a man holds a fork is something that can bother me. In that moment I thought I may have been the most shallow person in the world. However, had my date not done it, I would have never known this about myself. You will be surprised to find out things about yourself you probably never knew all because you took the time to open up to a stranger and noticed something about yourself you never noticed before. Remember, your dates should be fun, not perfect! So expect to notice things that you hadn't before. Also, remember to always be kind. While the way my date held his fork bothered me, I never brought it up. I simply took note about myself.

Dating is a numbers game for women too. Men understand that dating is a numbers game. I hate to break it to you but men who date multiple women better their chances of ending up with a woman they really want to be with. Putting "all your eggs in one basket" so to speak, is not the way to go. Dating only one person when you are single is setting yourself up for disappointment. If your ONE date doesn't work out, you end up feeling not only hurt but like a failure. The experience will lead you to date less. Remember, until you are in an established relationship where both of you agree to date exclusively, **you are single** and free to date multiple men. And you should.

Finally, dating several people means you never get caught up fantasizing about marrying the first person you date. Dating several people allows you to find the person who is most compatible with you. Dating multiple people means you are dating with clarity. You will start to really narrow down what personality traits are compatible with your personality. You will start to seek out those traits in the men you date. Basically, you will not simply settle for the first man who comes along and pays attention to you.

BE MORE THAN A PRETTY PACKAGE

We all like being pretty. We like to be dressed up and looking our best. We like to wear our hottest outfit with our best makeup and hair. However, women have to understand that being attractive is not just physical. There are a lot of pretty women in the world and now with the wide availability of makeup, hair, and clothing options, being "pretty" is getting easier and easier to be. It is important when you are dating to be more than just "pretty." Be interesting. Be funny. Be learned. Be more than just a well put together package. Yes, usually men do approach women based on a physical attraction. However, a man doesn't ask you out to only look at you all night. A man asks you out to actually get to know you. The truth is, if all you have to offer is your physical appearance, your date is not going to go very well. A man will only stare at you for so long before he finds something else to stare at that will capture his attention. Capturing attention is one thing, keeping attention is another.

It is very difficult to get the concept of "pretty isn't everything" across to women. In general, our society teaches girls and women to focus so hard on their appearance that they tend not to focus on developing the more important things about themselves...their minds, their personalities, their talents... Often women, especially physically attractive women, wonder why they never get asked on a second date. They never question whether they were boring or perhaps that they had nothing interesting to share about themselves. Often pretty women are stuck on being pretty, instead of being focused on being a well-rounded person, or even just focused on being a better person. Being physically attractive is great, but it is not the reason people like you. People like you because of who you are, not what you look like.

Remember, you must be more than just a pretty face. If you aren't interesting, men are not going to be interested in you. You must be more than just a "wrapping." You have to give your date more than just an appearance. You have to give your date something to get to know. You must also give yourself a chance to know them. Which leads to...

Be a good listener

Not only do you need to be interesting, you need to be interested. Dating is the opportunity for two people to get to know each other. Remember there are two of you on the date. The date is not just about you. There are two people getting to know each other. Take time to learn about the guy sitting across from you. Ask about his background, his likes and dislikes. Ask about his family. Give yourself the opportunity to learn. You may find out you have the same interests; you may find out you like his voice; you may find out you don't find him attractive at all but he is perfect for your friend. By being a good listener you will find out about him. And that's very important.

PUT YOUR PHONE DOWN

Yes, we live in the digital era. Smart phones are as attached to us as our legs. We are so "plugged in" we forget how to "tune in" when we are around other people. I am totally guilty of always having my phone in my hand. However, I put my phone away when on a date. Calls, texts, social media, are a distraction and will prevent you from really getting to know the guy you are on a date with.

Yes, your girlfriends will want updates (especially if he is "fine") but they will have to wait until the date is over (or at least until your date goes to the bathroom). Twitter and Facebook do not need to know that you are on a date. In fact, as a general rule, keep your dating life off of social media. (More on that in Chapter 8). Do not post pictures of you with your date, just don't. We live in an era of oversharing. People post pictures together much too soon. The world does not need to know who you are dating. Posting to social media while on your date is just bad manners. Sure, it's fun to share your experiences with your "friends" but focusing on your date is the only way to truly enjoy his company, so put the phone away.

RESIST THE URGE TO "CYBERSTALK"

Again, we live in a digital era, so of course we are going to Google the new guy. We are also going to check out all of his social networking pages if he has them. It's our new "normal." However, you must resist the urge to cyberstalk him. For example, if you are checking out every woman he follows or whose picture he "liked" you are cyberstalking and may quite possibly be showing some deep insecurities. The truth is you will not know everything there is to know about a man by what you find online. Yes, an online check can help you know if he's wanted for murder but outside of obvious dangers, try not to dig up his entire life story online. Allow him to let you know who he is by getting to know him in person instead.

Flirting is a skill. To some it comes naturally but for the most part it's practice. One of the biggest mistakes people make when trying to flirt is thinking that flirting has to do with finding a way to get the other person to be interested in you. In reality flirting has everything to do with making the other person feel good about themselves. When you get a person to feel good about themselves, they automatically like you more. Think about it. Who doesn't want to be around someone who makes them feel good?

Flirting takes practice to master. (This is another reason why dating as many men as possible will help you; it will give you multiple opportunities to practice your flirting skills). There are three basic techniques that will help you get started. It is important to note that in order to become a master at flirting you really have to learn what works for you. Over time the more dates you go on the more you will begin to understand what your strengths are. Everyone is different. For example, you might be very funny or even a great storyteller. However, these three techniques are no-brainers that everyone can do.

- Eye contact: Seems simple enough but I cannot tell you the amount of times women will not look men in the eyes. Do not hide your face. Look him in the eye. Holding someone's gaze is very powerful and it makes the other person feel like you are really listening to them. It's not staring though. Staring might make you seem crazy. It is genuine eye contact. If a man is talking to you, look him in the eyes as you listen. Another important thing about eye contact is that if you are talking to someone and they are being dishonest with you, they will have a hard time maintaining eye contact. Always watch out for dishonesty, it's a red flag.

- Smile: Yes, smiling is flirting. Smiling makes you feel good. Smiling is also contagious. When you smile it shows you are having a good time. When a man makes you smile he will always think, "She's likes me." Men like women who like them. Don't fake smile though. That will make you appear unstable. Only smile when it is genuine. But, be sure to smile.

- Compliment him: Making someone else feel good about themselves really does endear them to you. It's what flirting is all about, making the other person feel good. So find something about your date that you like, his eyes, his hands, his watch, whatever, and let him know. I promise he will smile too.

Sometimes women imitate what they think is sexy or flirting, such as flipping their hair or dancing what they believe is seductive. Sure you may think your hair flip or dance is sexy but if men don't respond to it, it's probably not sexy, seductive, or flirtatious. There is a good chance it's creepy. Yes, women can be creepy too. So make sure you are all brushed up on your flirting skills. Keep practicing on your dates. Learn what works for you and what doesn't. If one guy responds to you, there is a great chance that another guy will too. Eventually you will understand your own flirting techniques and become a master at them to the point that you will learn how to make them work for you.

BE A STORYTELLER

Flirting can get a conversation going, however, dating does require you to interact with your date beyond just listening to him. You need to be able to share something about yourself. Since I am an introvert, talking about myself is very difficult. Having a small arsenal of stories about yourself is very helpful, childhood stories, crazy dating stories, funny family stories, things that help a person understand you a bit more and also give you something that you can talk about without having to think too hard. I have learned that sharing quirky stories about my childhood is a very good tactic. It can help you if there is an awkward silence, plus people love to hear about your life. That's why people watch so much reality TV. People are naturally curious. And, here is a secret. You can recycle your stories with other dates. It's like having a conversation cheat book. If you are nervous or just awkward at the art of conversation, having a few stories about yourself can really help you. However, please note, share only the funny or endearing stories. Do not take this as an opportunity to complain about your life. Complaints are not endearing; they will have the complete opposite affect.

"FEAST OR FAMINE"

As you begin to learn how to date I want you to understand that dating has its ups and downs, the "feast or famine" phenomenon as I like to call it. This phenomenon happens to both men and women. If you don't know what I mean let me explain. For some reason while you navigate the dating world you are going to have times where you will suddenly get more male attention than you can handle, a "feast" of attention. During the "feast" times for some reason your phone will just be on fire. Out of nowhere men will be hitting you from your past. (I would really love to study this phenomenon. It's as though they all get the same signal at the same time) and new guys will be showing up seeking your attention. It is all very strange but I know from talking to my friends, both male and female, that I am not the only one to experience this. I don't know what causes it but I know it happens. And in turn just like the "feast" there will be times when you are in a "famine." Your phone will be desert dry...no calls, texts, tweets, nada... just no interest from anyone, anywhere. I am sharing this with you so that you understand that just because you are in a "famine" it doesn't mean something is wrong with you. It is just the ebb and flow of dating. It's normal. So ride the waves. If you are in a "famine" take that time to focus on yourself. And when you hit the "feast" just enjoy it but don't get upset because it doesn't last. Get used to the ups and downs of dating. There will be times when there are no dates, and then there will be times when there are too many.

If you are unhappy because you are single, you are going to stay single and unhappy. Your happiness should never be dependent on something outside of yourself. If you are looking for someone else to complete you, you will always be incomplete. Happiness and fulfillment should never come from someone other than yourself. The truth is people who are successful at dating are people who are already happy in their own skin without relying on anyone else.

I know society teaches us that something is wrong with a woman if she is single. That is simply not true. Being single is not a disease or debilitation. Being single is just fine. I know the world looks at single women, especially if she is over thirty and has no kids, as some sort of plague that has hit the earth, but there are plenty of happy, single women in this world. Before you beat yourself up for not being married or in a relationship know that married women tend to be unhappier than single women. "[A]ccording to research, the average married woman is less happy than the average married man, less happy than single women, less convinced that married people are happier than single people, and more likely to file for divorce. Once returned to single life, women's happiness recovers, whereas men's declines, and divorced women are less eager to remarry than divorced men."[2] So, before you jump to believe marriage or a relationship will make you happier try being happy with the life you have now. Right now you are living for you, living life and enjoying it without feeling any of the world's judgment. This should be the goal, to be happy as you are, always.

Additionally, if you are unhappy single you will also be unhappy in a relationship. Happiness does not come from something outside of yourself, it comes from inside of you. Contrary to popular belief, you do not need another person to "complete you." You are a complete person as you are. So be happy. You are deserving of happiness. Plus, no one wants to date an unhappy person. Being unhappy is a sure way to stay single.

[2] Wade, Lisa. (2017, January 10). *The Modern Marriage Trap — and What to Do About It.* http://time.com/money/4630251/the-modern-marriage-trap-and-what-to-do-about-it/

CHAPTER 5: LET'S TALK ABOUT MEN

MEN ARE INSECURE WHEN IT COMES TO WOMEN

Sorry guys, I know your secret. Most men are insecure when it comes to women. It only takes a moment to figure this out if you really think about what men do just to secure the attention of women. Men are quick to talk about how women dress, wear their hair, put on makeup to get the attention of men but take a moment to think about what men do to get the attention of women. Men will change their whole lives for women. They get better jobs, drive better cars, and even adorn themselves with expensive clothes, watches and other jewelry, because just by doing these things, it makes them more attractive to women. Men, in fact, do a lot more to gain women's attention than women do to gain men's attention.

Think about it ladies, how many times have you pushed yourself forward in your career and thought about all the men who were going to like you more because you have a better job? Never done that? Well, it's not really a thing women do. But why do so many men work so hard to better themselves? Women are a big reason. Why? Because men feel insecure in their social status and attractiveness to women. Men know that a better job, which leads to more money, can make women find them more attractive. Men with more money have greater chances of meeting and dating the woman they really want. And men know this.

Ladies, just knowing men are insecure when it comes to women gives you an advantage. Suddenly you will see that while many men seem confident, somewhere inside of him is a guy not sure if you will like him, because deep down inside he may not feel that he is enough or has enough, to hold your attention. Remember this as you date. You will start to notice male insecurity more and more.

In a recent conversation, a man told me that times have changed and women are now pursuing men, that women now ask him out, that he no longer had to chase women and he wouldn't be doing so. I was very amused by this conversation. While times have changed and women are more bold about asking men out and letting men know how they feel, this isn't how humans have been socially conditioned. (I was also amused because he was still pursuing me).

Since men have held more positions of power, many more so than women, and because women generally look for men who can "provide" (again social conditioning), men go after the woman they are interested in. He makes it known to the woman, letting her know what he can give to her, presenting his "feathers" so to speak, in order to show his worthiness of her affection. Now, this may seem a sexist and archaic statement but seriously, women are socially conditioned to choose from the potential mates who make their interests known, and men are conditioned to pursue the woman who interests them. I know people will want to debate me on this but that's a scientific discussion for another day. It may seem the opposite way at this point in our social development with so many women competing for male attention, but no matter how much attention a man gets, men still go after the woman they really want. Keep this in mind when you are dating; **men chase, women choose.**

Always remember that as a woman you are the "chooser." Simply put, I don't care how cute he is, if he smiled at you, or if he is exactly "what you want" in a guy. **Do not chase him.** If a man likes you, he will let you know. I have never chased after a guy in my whole dating life, ever. Why? Because I understand something about men, they always go after who they want. They are hardwired to do so. No matter the obstacles, no matter the challenges, if a man really likes you he will find a way to let you know. Even if you aren't single, as many married women can attest, if a man likes you he will let you know. Trust me on this one. If he doesn't let his interest in you be known, then he probably isn't interested in you. Don't feel bad, it happens. Not every man is going to want to date you. That's life. Do not take it personally. Maybe he isn't attracted to you; maybe he is madly in love with someone; you just don't know. If he does not show interest do not try to force it. **Only pay attention to the men who pay attention to you.**

There is another reason why I say do not chase men. Male egos tend to really get off on women chasing them. It is a major ego stroker for a man to have a woman chase him. It's flattering and amusing. Think about how guys laugh at women who fight over them. Clearly the man isn't truly interested in either woman or else he would not allow them to fight. A man who is truly in love with a woman would never allow another woman to harm her. The problem with chasing men is that they are usually not seriously interested in the women who chase them. They just enjoy the attention and antics. It is entertainment, something for them to pass time with. Don't be a man's entertainment. You will get hurt in the end because he is using you and you will not end up with what you want.

MEN MAKE TIME FOR WHO THEY WANT

Read it again: **Men make time for who they want**. There are no ifs, ands, or buts about this statement. If a man really wants you, he will find the time to spend with you. This is a mistake many women make, myself included. If you only hear from a guy when he wants something (sex usually) but he never has time to see you when you want to see him, he isn't truly interested in being with you. He does not make time for you not because he is "busy," he doesn't make time for you because you are not a priority to him. His interest level is not high. Stop thinking he's too busy for you, because no matter if he's a CEO of a Fortune 500 company, or a guy who manages the local pizzeria, if he likes you, he will find the time to see you, point blank. Even Barrack Obama makes time for Michelle, because he loves her. Women often like to make excuses in their minds as to why the guy they are interested in hasn't seen or communicated with them. The truth is, if he really wanted to see or talk to you, he would.

Men like spending time with the woman they are interested in. They will move mountains to do so. Do not waste time on a guy who doesn't make time for you. If he doesn't call or does not want to hang out with you, he is not interested, (or he is seeing someone else)! Focus your interests on a guy who does call and who does have time for you. I do understand that sometimes it is hard to let go, (More about letting go in Chapter 9), however, stop wasting your life waiting on someone who really just is not all that interested in you.

When you first start dating a man, you are not dating him, you are dating what I like to call his "representative." The "representative" is a man on his "best" behavior until he is comfortable enough to show his "true" self. I won't say this is men trying to be deceptive, but instead, men trying to show you their best side at least for the first 3-5 dates. Until a man is completely comfortable with you expect to get to know his representative. His true personality will eventually make its way out. Usually the representative and true personality are not drastically different from one another to the point where it's a problem, however, don't expect the personality of the representative forever. A lot of women are shocked when there is a change in the guy they have dated for a while. This is normal, so remember, do not fall for the "representative." Wait until the "real" guy shows up. He's in there waiting for the "right" time to come out. That's usually when he thinks you are all in to him. Meeting the real guy is when you will be able to really judge a man's level of interest and also see any red flags. (More on red flags later in this chapter).

Men can be interested in you for different reasons. Sometimes there are men who only want to have sex with you. Sometimes they are interested in settling down. Sometimes they are interested in dating you short-term. Sometimes men actually want to be just friends. (Yes, some men want to be just friends with you). The question is how do you know which level of interest a man has in you?

You have to be able to read a man's signals. The easiest signals to pick up on are the sexual ones. If a man just wants sex he will pretty much be up front about it at the beginning, no representative needed. He is going to make remarks about your body and what he'd like to do with you sexually, etc. Women often think that a man who is interested in a sexual relationship with them means that the man wants more, or that eventually he will want more than a sexual relationship. This is not the case. When a woman gets involved in what should be only a sexual relationship and then becomes more emotionally attached than the man, she ends up hurt because the man doesn't reciprocate these emotional feelings. Sometimes it's the guy who gets hurt, even when he initiates the sexual relationship. If you are not prepared for a sexual only relationship, **do not get involved** with a guy who is sending you sex only relationship signals.

What about the signals that he wants more than just sex? Remember what I said before. The signals you are looking for in the beginning are respect, engagement, and interest. A man who is looking for more than just sex is going to make sure he comes at you in the best way possible. Sure a man who is interested in you will also be interested in you sexually, but his respect for you will keep his base behavior at bay. He is going to make sure you know his "representative" well, so that he makes a good impression on you.

Men who have longer-term interests in you will ask you about your plans for the future. They will ask you about your thoughts on marriage, children, religion, etc. All the things that deal with thoughts about the future will come up in conversation. Some men will even say up front they want to settle down soon. Don't get too excited about this statement if he says it early, it just means that is what he is looking for. That does not necessarily mean he wants to settle down with you. In fact, it is possible that you may have zero interest in settling down with him. A man talking and asking about future possibilities is simply a signal as to the level of his interest, meaning it is more than just sex. Men who have longer-term interests in you will also make plans for the next date.

If the date is going well and a man is very interested in seeing you again, he will try to get on your calendar as soon as possible. However, if a man is not interested in seeing you again or only slightly interested, you will get the "I will call/text/hit you later" comment. Never take this personally. Not everyone will be interested in you. Rejection is a part of life and the better you are at moving on and letting go when rejected, the better you will be at dating (I will talk about this more in Chapter 9). Remember, dating is a numbers game. So what, one guy isn't interested in you. There are still thousands more. Keep it moving. If you are following my advice, you probably already have another date planned with another guy in the immediate future. Another reason to date multiple people at the same time, if one guy doesn't work out, you already have another to look forward too. Keep it moving!

I have already mentioned that the "good guy" thing is a fallacy so let's get that thought out of your head and get you to start thinking, "Is he good for me?" That's more important. One way to know if someone isn't good for you is to **not ignore the red flags**.

Let's talk a moment about the type of men to avoid. You have been on a few dates with a great "representative" and then the "real" guy shows up. Yes, we all want to date a great guy but often we ignore the red flags that are waving blatantly in our faces, especially after meeting the "representative" who was "so nice" and "so perfect" (or maybe even the red flags showed up in the beginning). Listen, red flags are red flags for a reason. They are there to warn us to stop and reverse course. If you see a red flag, or anything that makes you uncomfortable, **stop dating him!** You will save yourself a lot of problems later on. Most of the problems women have in dating stem from ignoring the red flags we see in the beginning. I am guilty of this as well. If you see the red flags, leave him alone!

Low Self-Esteem - Yes, men suffer from low self-esteem too. Often we hear about women with low self-esteem, but men also suffer from low self-esteem and poor self-image. Dating a man with low self-esteem and poor self-image can lead you into an abusive relationship. The problem with dating a man with low self-esteem is he seeks out women to compensate for his own lack of self-worth. Suddenly you become his self-worth and whenever he is feeling low, it will be "your" fault.

An interesting thing about men with low self-esteem is how the symptoms of it manifest. Many times the low self-esteem is not obvious, however, if he does not seem comfortable in his own skin and makes a point of constantly elevating himself above other people, there are definitely some self-esteem issues going on. If he constantly points out how he is better/greater/smarter than someone/something else or he would have done a better job at something than someone else, you can bet there are some self-esteem/self-image issues going on because people who are comfortable with themselves do not make a point of telling other people how much "better" they are than others. You may even find that he will try to compete with you, or is uncomfortable if you get more attention, or more of the "spotlight" than he does.

The other way the low self-esteem man shows up is as the "playboy." Men who are "playboys" are classic examples of men suffering from low self-esteem. Usually these men grew up without a positive male role model and equate "masculinity" with having a lot of women. The constant stream of women is compensating for their own diminished self-esteem. Without women they feel of little value. Playboys may seem like the most confident men on the planet, however, without the women to keep their self-worth bolstered, they are extremely fragile. Steer clear.

Another indicator of low self-esteem is often masked in a hyper (read toxic) masculine package. Yes, that extremely "manly man" probably has low self-esteem. Notice a sexist attitude? That is one of the most common elements of low self-esteem in men. They have a need to subjugate women to feel better about themselves. If you find yourself around a man who constantly has a need to talk about how women "should" be, or a man who constantly makes comments about how women "should look," or how men are "in charge" and that's the way it "should be," just a constant stream of sexist comments, steer clear. There is a self-esteem issue hidden somewhere in there.

Hyper/Toxic/Masculinity can also be an indicator of closeted homosexuality. Often men who have problems with accepting their sexual orientation overcompensate by becoming more of what they believe is "masculine."

Men Who Disparage Or Constantly Talk About Their Ex-Girlfriend(s) - If the man you are dating constantly disparages his ex or exes, or if he constantly "elevates" you above his ex, or if he just constantly talks about his ex, steer clear. A man who constantly puts down his ex is showing he isn't over the pain of his last relationship. By constantly talking about her, he is also showing his lack of interest in you. Basically you become a way for him to talk about his former relationship/s. Don't be that woman. He needs to work through his issues with his past.

A man who constantly elevates you while also disparaging his ex is using a psychological "divide and conquer" technique. The "divide and conquer" technique once you understand it, you will notice over and over, and be able to identify in other situations. By elevating one over the other he makes each feel that she must constantly have to compete to stay "different" from the other, thereby becoming controllable. If you encounter a man who uses this tactic, run.

Men Who Disparage Their Child's/Children's Mother - Any man who would disparage his child's mother to you will eventually disparage you. I actually stopped seeing a man for this very reason. A man who would put down the mother of his child to a woman he is dating shows a total lack of care for his own children. I don't care how "crazy" his child's mother may be. Even if it is true, a caring man just does not disparage his children's mother, especially not to his date. The love of his children (which is the strongest love of all in my world), would not allow him to put you in a position to feel as though you could put down the mother of his children. If you run into this type of man just remember, if he will treat the mother of his children this way, he will treat you just as badly down the line.

Men Who Use Backhanded Compliments - Beware of men who try to "take you down a notch." They say things like "You are pretty but..." or "I like you but not when..." These are psychological tactics that make a person become easier to control. This is also a BIG indicator of a controlling man, quite possibly an abusive one. The first thing he does is tear you down so he can "build you up" to what he thinks you should be, which makes the woman who is his victim constantly in need of reassurance from him. If a man can never pay you an outright compliment without him saying something hurtful on the back end, steer clear.

Men Who Disappear - Things are going great and then *poof* he disappears. Suddenly you can't get in touch with him, no calls, no texts, nothing. Just as suddenly he reappears, with a plausible excuse. The disappearing act usually indicates the guy you are dating is already in a relationship. He disappears because he is with his girlfriend or his **wife.** No, he is not just "busy." No, he does not need time. Do not fall for this trick. Remember what I said before, men make time for who they want. If he isn't making time for you, he isn't really interested and if he keeps disappearing you are not a priority to him. The person he is disappearing with is his priority. You are just something for him to entertain himself with. Do not be his entertainment. Keep it moving.

Jealous/Controlling/Possessive Men - A man who is strangely possessive, controlling, or jealous right from the beginning is a big red flag. If he gets upset because a man smiles at you or is asking for the passcode to your phone, he is showing signs of an abusive personality and a deep insecurity. A big indicator of a man who has jealousy issues is a man who wants you to post pictures of him on your social media accounts. He wants the world to know that you are "taken." Men like this should be avoided. Do not get involved with men like this. You could end up in a potentially dangerous situation.

Dishonest Men - Anytime you find out a man has lied to you, that is a huge red flag. Dishonest people cannot be trusted, ever, and usually someone who will lie to you about something small will also lie about something big. Omissions are also lies. A man omitting something big like, for example, he has four children instead of just the two he told you about, is being dishonest with you. Do not ignore this red flag. Dishonesty will always lead to issues down the line. Whenever you find out a man is not being honest with you, move on. Do not be forgiving, that is a mistake women make over and over. Drop him immediately. You are worth being with someone who is honest with you. Do not settle for someone who thinks it is ok to deceive you.

Emotional Manipulation- Any type of emotional manipulation is a red flag. I talk more about emotional manipulation tactics later in this chapter.

If you are a man reading this book, I do not say this to insult you, but it's true, men are simple creatures. Men are so simple, in fact, that it doesn't take a lot to understand exactly what they are thinking and want when it comes to dating. Just pay attention to what they say and do. A man who is interested in you will always show you his level of interest. A man who only wants to have sex with you will only make sexual advances towards you. A man who only wants to be friends with you will only do friend activities with you. Men generally are open books about what they want. I am not sure where the complexity came in for women trying to figure out what men want. They want what they say from the start. Men really are not that beguiling. For example, men who want marriage will say so early. So, if that's what you are looking for and a man tells you he doesn't want to get married, move on. Do not think you can change his mind. He won't because that is not what he wants. Simply put men are not that complex. Stop looking for hidden messages where there aren't any. Listen to what he says and pay attention to what he does. You will get all the information that you need.

Men often overestimate their abilities while women tend to underestimate theirs. This is something Sheryl Sandberg touched on in her book, "Lean In." She says, "[Women] consistently underestimate ourselves. Multiple studies in multiple industries show that women often judge their own performance as worse than it actually is, while men judge their own performance as better than it actually is."[3] What does this mean? This means that men seem way more confident, even when it comes to dating. In reality, they are feeling the same unsure feelings as you are, but they tend to mask them better because they have had more practice masking their feelings. That means they are hoping you will call or text them just as you are hoping they will call or text you. Even the stereotypical "playboy" who seems to have all the confidence in the world, may deep down inside be the most unsure. Remember this when you are feeling unsure of yourself on a date; your date is feeling unsure too.

[3] Sandberg, Sheryl. *Lean In.* New York. Alfred A. Knopf, 2013. Print.

Men, in general, also have an inflated view of themselves. This is why even men who are seemingly physically unattractive seem to believe they are "God's gift to women." (Sexism contributes greatly to this as well). However, knowing that men generally fake confidence is something that women can and should take advantage of while dating. People do not talk much about this but women provide men reassurance of their confidence. For example, the stereotypical playboy needs the admiration of multiple women to feel good about himself. Without this constant attention from women he will feel he has no value and his self-esteem suffers. Think about it, men seek out better employment, vehicles, clothes, jewelry, just to impress women. They will say it is because they "like" those things, however, most things men do are just to gain the attraction of women and the admiration of men, who see the type of women the man attracts. Men also benefit more from marriage and relationships than women because women provide more of the "mental labor" and support in relationships than men do.

In other words, you as the woman already start out with the upper hand because you are not going into dates with inflated confidence. Remember that a man has more to gain from your interaction with him than you do. Knowing this will help you feel more confident in the beginning. Not only will it help your confidence, knowing this fact will help you notice the little 'tells' that a man has which show his insecurities. Pay attention. The little things matter. When you notice a man's nervousness and insecurities take that as an opportunity to comfort him. Showing you care makes you more attractive and when he feels more comfortable around you he will open up more. The more open you both become the better the interaction.

MEN ARE EMOTIONAL

Yes, I said it. Men are emotional. In fact, men feel emotion more deeply than women. I know the men reading this are screaming, "No that's not true!" (...because you men are emotional...). It is. Science has proven this. Male babies are born more emotive than female babies. "[I]nfant boys are more emotionally reactive than girls. They display more positive as well as negative affect, focus more on the mother, and display more . . . distress and demands for contact than do girls."[4] Male toddlers express more

---

4 "The Fragile Male." BMJ : British Medical Journal 321.7276 (2000): 1609–1612. Print.

emotion than female toddlers. Men are more likely to harm women if they are rejected. Why? Because men are more emotional. The reason why men appear less emotional is because we live in a male dominated society and they are socially conditioned to believe that expressing emotions is a feminine trait and so they are taught to mask how they feel. Men often have a very hard time expressing how they are feeling because they were only taught to repress their emotions. This is also why men are more prone to express anger when hurt. They have not learned how to express their pain in an emotionally healthy way. However, just because they do not express how they feel, does not mean they don't feel. They do, and very deeply. Keep this in mind as you navigate dating. If you hurt a man's feelings be prepared for him to hold it against you for a very long time.

For those men reading this book who are screaming that women are more emotional, the fact is, women are not more emotional than men. Women are more likely to express their emotions than men. Women are better at emotional expression because we have reached emotional maturity. We were allowed to express our emotions as children and teens without being taught something was wrong with us for being "emotional." That is why we are more comfortable expressing our emotions more openly than men. It does not mean we are more emotional. Emotional is verbally and/or physically attacking a woman you never met because she refused your advances; that's emotional. Women don't do that.

Although it is rarely discussed, because men are emotional, they form very deep attachments to women. Remember, men benefit from relationships and marriage more than women. Women in relationships generally help men in dealing with their emotions. We become the vehicle through which a man learns to emotionally express himself. Once a man is attached to you emotionally, it is very difficult for him to let go. Be aware of this as you date. Do not allow a man to become emotionally attached to you if you are not seriously interested in him. An emotionally attached man can become an issue for you later.

MEN ARE MASTERS OF EMOTIONAL MANIPULATION

Strangely, although men are more emotional, they are also more practiced at emotional manipulation. Somewhere along the way in our society we all have been conditioned to believe that emotionally abusive behaviors in relationships are "normal." And those behaviors have everything to do with manipulation. These manipulative behaviors also benefit men more than women. I am not sure how men got to be so good at emotional manipulation but they are, and for some reason women are less aware of it. What is the point of emotional manipulation? Control. The fact is sexism has created an environment where men being in "control" over women and what they do is "normal." What you never want to do in your dating life is lose control. Losing control can cause you to end up in a position of unhappiness and confusion. Dating is supposed to be fun, not draining. Many women have bad dating experiences because they confuse manipulation for "love." It is difficult to know the difference, especially when our whole lives we have been conditioned to believe that possession and control equate to love.

I saw a tweet one day from a man telling other men that the way to get to an attractive woman is to insult her. Basically, his suggestion was to take a shot at her confidence, because when a guy takes a woman down a notch she is easier to get to. (Remember our previous discussion, Red flags, Backhanded Compliments). He was right of course. This manipulation technique does work. (It also works on men). In fact, most people are susceptible to this technique because a person who is unsure will constantly second guess themselves and become more easily controlled, looking to the person who is manipulating them to reassure their confidence. I am telling you this because once you are aware of this technique, it doesn't work. You will recognize it immediately when a man tries it on you. Usually, if a man tries this, it means leave him alone immediately. (You can also give him a backhanded compliment on the way out the door. It generally stuns them).

Another emotionally manipulative tactic that many men use is putting you into a guilt trip, defensive position, or accusing you of doing something that they, in fact, are doing. For example, you decide to go out with your girlfriends one night. Suddenly the guy is "acting funny" or stops speaking to you to make you feel bad. This form of manipulation puts you in the position of appearing to be the bad guy when you have done nothing wrong. You are not the bad guy, he is. Sulky men are manipulators. Do not waste your time with a man who cannot tell you he is upset with you, even if he is only upset because he feels insecure. Mature men are up front when something bothers them. Men who will sulk or put a guilt trip on you are operating on a child's level. You do not want to date a child. If he sulks or pouts or becomes sullen out of nowhere, recognize the emotional manipulation and leave him alone.

Another example of this manipulation tactic is when a man accuses you of behaviors that he is actually exhibiting. For example, a man will accuse you of arguing with him all the time, when in fact, he is the person who initiates the argument. This is an attempt to make you defend yourself when you have no reason to. Again, you are not the bad guy, he is. Never take a defensive stance when faced with this type of manipulation. As soon as you start defending yourself when you have no reason to, you will lose and fall victim to the manipulation. Instead redirect the conversation back to the actual issue, or just ignore the behavior. Either way, do not defend yourself when you have no reason to. Start to pay attention to manipulative behaviors; when you start recognizing them, they begin not to affect you.

Gaslighting is one of the most damaging manipulation tactics, and one of the hardest to recognize. It is also a male favorite. Gaslighting, if you are not familiar with it, is when you tell someone that something bothers you and they downplay or ignore your feelings. They make it seem as though your feelings have no validity. Be cognizant of this manipulation tactic. If a man doesn't acknowledge your feelings, leave him alone. This tactic is a way of diminishing your emotions and position and eventually controlling you. "Why are you making this a big deal?" or "You're being crazy!" or "I don't know what you are talking about," are things men say when they are gaslighting you. Often women start to second-guess whether their feelings are valid when faced with gaslighting. Men are very practiced at gaslighting. I think that is because our society has normalized this behavior for men. Sexism makes it acceptable. That is why men find it so easy to call a woman "crazy" when she is doing something he doesn't like. She is not "crazy," meaning she has some type of real mental health issue, she is just not behaving in a way that he wants her to. So she's "crazy" because she is not in his control.

The truth is your feelings are very valid and when a man refuses to acknowledge them he is manipulating you. I was involved with more than one gaslighter. I didn't recognize it. Later, I would start to second-guess myself. I then would stop vocalizing when something bothered me. I basically became controlled. That's what gaslighting is intended to do. The manipulation will lead you to a point where you will stop vocalizing how you feel and that makes the man comfortable. He now has what he wants and you will continue to be placed in discomfort. Being in relationships with people who were gaslighting me ended up with me feeling bad about myself and getting depressed. I did not recognize that I was being manipulated and controlled. It took me years to understand how damaging gaslighting/manipulation is, and to also recover from the damage it caused my self-esteem. That is why I want you to be aware of this type of manipulation and learn how to recognize it, because you can avoid a lot of heartache and pain if you do. Remember, anytime you see manipulation tactics, steer clear.

MEN ARE COMPETITIVE

Men are competitive. They are socially conditioned to be competitive. In general, most men want to win. This is a big reason why dating multiple men at the same time is an advantage for you. If it is known that you are dating more than just one man, the men who are genuinely interested in you will take it on as a challenge and try to beat out the other men. Think about it. How often do we see celebrity men squabbling over the same woman? It is in their nature to compete for the woman they genuinely want. This also means that the men who were only somewhat interested in you will not invest the time pursuing you. They aren't interested in being a part of the competition.

Dating several men at the same time is also a great way to weed out the guys who are only slightly interested in you. And while this book is not about finding a serious relationship or husband, dating multiple men is a great method to do just that. You will not only up your chances of finding a man who is the most compatible with you, you will also find a man who is interested in you more than all of the others. A lot of women may be put off by me suggesting this because patriarchy and sexism have taught them that, "Women aren't like that." However, this book is about dating, having fun, and being happy. For the record, women are "like that." We have always been like that. We are perfectly capable of dating more than one man at once and enjoying the experience. And we should. So, do not be afraid to take advantage of men's competitive nature. You are doing yourself a favor.

CHAPTER 6: WHAT ABOUT SEX?

YOUR GREATEST ASSET IS NOT YOUR VAGINA

Let that sink in for a moment. *Your greatest asset is not your vagina.* You as a woman bring far more "to the table" than sex. Many of you will have a hard time understanding and accepting this concept, but it is one thing you must learn or "unlearn" to have a fulfilling and happy dating life. To understand why our society acts as though women have less value because they may or may not have had more than one sexual partner, you really have to analyze sexism and how it impacts women.

From the moment little girls can walk they are taught to protect what is perceived as a woman's greatest asset, her virginity. Little girls are shamed for their dresses being short or accidentally blowing up.

One day a woman stopped me in a Target because my daughter was riding on the cart and she could see my daughter's underwear, and she "wanted to let me know." This one act from a stranger, who thought she was helping actually upset my daughter. The woman upset me too. My daughter felt that she had done something wrong and I had to explain to her that she had done nothing wrong. That is how sexism works. Sexism makes girls and women feel that there is something wrong with our bodies and our sexuality. That is how sexism maintains control over what people think about women, and their bodies, and their sex lives. The truth is, there is nothing wrong with our bodies and there is nothing wrong with our sex lives. Had I had a son instead of a daughter I doubt that the woman would have said anything at all. Sexism is perpetuated onto women not only by men, but by women too. That is why it is still in place today. Sexism is part of the reason 60% of white women voted for Trump. Sexism has a strong hold on the minds of women, so strong that women teach sexist ideas to girls.

Because of sexism, not only are girls taught there is something "shameful" about their bodies from the time they are toddlers to make them feel uncomfortable, girls and women are also taught to "protect" their virginity and their vaginas as if that is the most precious and valuable thing about them. Women must always "wait" until the "right" time to lose their virginity. In fact, the world teaches girls and women that our vaginas are so special, so much so that losing your virginity as a woman has to be to someone "special" and "worthy" of such a "precious gift." So much emphasis is placed on a woman's virginity that often girls are left heartbroken after the guy she chose as the "one and only" to lose her virginity to dumps her for the next opportunity to be inside a different vagina, which is ultimately what happens. It is rare that anyone goes on to be forever with the person they lost their virginity to. Even after the "virgin" heartbreak women continue to protect their "precious asset" well into adulthood, allowing only the most "worthy" to access it.

The problem with sexism is that girls and women are learning that the only asset they bring to dating is sex. They are under pressure to only date those who are "worthy" of their "asset" and if they do not protect their "asset" they will lose value. Of course, the opposite is true for men. Men losing their virginity is a rite of passage, something to be proud of. The more women men have sex with the more "manly" they become. Their "value" is not diminished by having sex;

it is increased. This is another reason men often have more fulfilling dating lives than women. They don't spend time worrying about their reputations, they do not have to. They can just simply, date.

Women spend so much time protecting their "reputations" (read that vaginas) that their whole dating lives often revolve around who got the "cookie," how many people got it, and whether her value is lessened because too many people had a chance to have the "cookie." And, they have to keep the "cookie" in the "cookie jar" for 90 days or else men won't respect them.

It's utterly ridiculous. You are more than what is between your legs. In fact, the less you think about what people think about who's been inside of your vagina the more you can think about what makes you happy. Trust me, not sharing your vagina is not going to make you happy. In fact, not sharing your vagina has a greater possibility of having the exact opposite effect. Sex is an important and vital part of the human experience. The truth is people who have active sex lives are happier.

To think that women have nothing more to offer when dating than their sexual and child-bearing capabilities is truly insulting if you really think about it. Forget about being intelligent, creative, or ambitious, it is your vagina where all of your value lies. I mean you are the best marketer in your marketing group but you had sex with Larry and Seymour, clearly you have no value now… It is insulting.

Women must recognize that sexism and misogyny affect us too, mentally, where it is most damaging. If you think your only value is sex, you will only offer sex as your dating asset. Think about that for a moment. The thing you protect, your vagina, is the only thing you are holding as valuable when you date…not your companionship, your intelligence, your humor…just your vagina, that's all you have to work with. If this has been your way of thinking it is a very good chance the men you dated knew this about you. It is also a good chance that once they got your "asset" they disappeared. So if you dated a man who seemed great but you refused to have sex with him for 90 days and then after the 90 days you finally had sex with him but you never heard from him again, guess what? The only thing of "value" you offered, he got, and now he is no longer interested.

I know it is difficult to unlearn something you've been taught your whole life, but knowing that your value is not changed because of the number of men you had sex with is really a freeing thing. Let go of sexism's control over your body. Stop feeling ashamed of your body. Stop feeling ashamed to be a woman with a healthy sex life. Stop thinking you have less value because you had sex. Stop allowing men to have that kind of power over your life. A man who likes you is going to date you no matter what. Your value to him is not based on your vagina. If it is, he has some growing up to do and you probably should not date him anyway.

Moving past sexism's hold on your sexuality is key to a fulfilling dating life. Only you can control your sexuality, not society. Do not let what other people "think" you should be or do, stop you from doing what you want to do. If you want to enjoy sex with someone, enjoy sex with someone. If you choose not to have sex with someone, do not have sex. The point is, it is your choice. Remember, men are never devalued because of multiple sexual partners. In fact, men often are praised for it. They are taught that their "value" goes up because they have multiple sexual partners. You have to recognize sexism for what it is, a system of control. If you make a woman believe she loses value, you make her easier to control.

In other words your sexuality, your vagina, is yours and yours alone. No one has any power to change anything about it or you. Your value is not connected to your vagina. Your value is in who you are, not in who you have sex with. Do not let sexism make you believe you have less worth because you choose to enjoy your sexuality. Do not allow society to control who you are. Do not let sexism decide your value.

WHY IT'S OK NOT TO HAVE A 90-DAY RULE

The 90-day rule is stupid. (You can tell Steve Harvey I said so). Again, the 90-day rule is stupid. It is an arbitrary rule someone came up with that sounded like a good idea for women who believe their only asset is their vagina. When to have sex is a personal decision between you and the person you decide to have sex with. You can do that whenever you want to…first date…second date…twentieth date… seventieth date…the point is, it is your choice as to when you will have sex with someone.

Waiting 90 days isn't going to do anything to make your interaction with a man any better or make him respect you more. Having sex on the first date will not harm you, or harm your chances of a second date, nor will it ruin your reputation (vagina) in any way. There are plenty of people who are married who had sex on the first date. If you have sex when it "feels right," and not when some sexist dude tells you to, you will be very happy. If the passion has hit you both, you are swept up in passionate kisses, and you have sex, whether it's the first date, the third, or twentieth, you both will be very very happy. The point to remember is, it is always your choice. It is your decision about when to have sex. Do not worry about what other people may think about you. Do not worry that the man you chose to have sex with won't value you anymore. If he thinks that by touching you or having sex with you his touch causes you to have less value, he probably shouldn't be touching you in the first place. Again, having sex does not make you less valuable. This is a falsehood placed on women to keep their sexuality under the control of men. Free yourself from this controlled thinking and begin to enjoy your sex life as you prefer it.

Having sex is also important to determining sexual compatibility. No matter how you try to swing it, sexual compatibility is highly important in a partnership. If you are looking to get involved in a serious relationship or marriage you need to be sexually compatible. It's more important to find out earlier than later whether you are sexually compatible with someone, especially if you plan to be with this person long-term. How awful would it be to date someone for three whole months, never having sex, only to discover three months down the line that the sex is horrible? You would be terribly disappointed that you wasted all that time with someone that you do not even want sexually. The truth is when there is no sexual compatibility there is no genuine interest, especially long-term. There are many women right now, who are in relationships or even married to men, who do not have a satisfying sex life. It is scary but many women think it is normal to not be satisfied sexually. It isn't.

Long gone are the days when men are the only ones satisfied in the bedroom. Being satisfied with your sex life is very important to your happiness. You deserve to enjoy sex just as much as a man does. If the sex isn't good, don't believe other non-sexual things will compensate for it in the relationship. Sexual compatibility is either there or it isn't. Many times people who aren't sexually compatible stay together only to end up miserable because they never get their own sexual needs met. This often leads to people having affairs to satisfy those needs. So instead of ending up in a situation where you are unhappy with your sex life, actively seek out a situation that is sexually satisfying as well.

GET A FRIEND WITH BENEFITS

If you are not familiar with this term "friend with benefits," it means having someone you are sexually compatible with, but you are not in a relationship with and have no intention of being in a serious relationship with. I know you may be freaking out a little bit. But, something the world doesn't teach women, unlike men, is to satisfy their sexual needs outside the confines of a relationship. You may have even had sex with a man that you were not in a relationship with thinking he was interested in more. He may have just used you, but don't feel bad, men understand that sex outside of a relationship is healthy. Take the lesson and use it yourself. I'm telling you that you have sexual needs and that you should satisfy them. Men do this all the time. You are human and humans are sexual beings with sexual needs. A healthy sex life (and safe one!) is good for you. It will help boost your mood and your confidence. Also, not satisfying your sexual needs will affect your judgement when it comes to dating. Many women make the mistake of thinking they really want to date the guy who isn't at all compatible with them just because they got caught up in one night of passionate sex after six plus months of their hormones raging. When your hormones are raging you will make less rational decisions. Hormones really do affect your judgement; they can trick you into believing you are in love when really you just had an orgasm for the first time in six months.

But, women get emotionally attached to men they have sex with right? You've probably heard that women can't have sex without being emotionally attached. You might have even told yourself that you cannot have sex with a guy you aren't emotionally connected to. Well, I'm here to tell you that is not true. It is quite possible for women to have sex without being emotionally attached. I'm not saying you won't care about the person you choose as a friend with benefits; you probably will actually care very much for him. That's why he is your "friend" in the first place. However, a good friend with benefits is the guy you like, but just don't really want to be in a relationship with. We all have those guys, the "He's cute but he's just my friend." You can't really put your finger on it but something about him doesn't rise to the level of relationship. Still he is more than just a "friend" to you. You just don't want to date him. Maybe you even cuddle with him (a good indicator of closeness), but you still don't "like him like that." That guy, yes, he is your "friend with benefits."

But, why would you want to engage in a sexual relationship with a guy you have no interest in seriously dating? A friend with benefits is useful for many reasons, first, of course, is satisfying your sexual urges, and it is much easier to date when you do not have raging hormones. You will be much clearer in your thought processes in terms of being able to get to really know the men you are going out with. Secondly, knowing that you can have sex anytime you want to will make you less likely to want to immediately jump into a relationship with the new guy you're dating. Often women want to immediately jump into a relationship with the first guy who has taken them out in months because they just want to have regular sex again. Thirdly, if you have a friend with benefits waiting for your "booty call" after your date, the new guy you're dating will only truly catch your eye if he sparks something deep inside of you that connects you to him. Finally, again, sex is healthy for you. It makes you feel good and it makes you exude confidence. A healthy sex life makes you look and feel more attractive. A sexually confident woman always attracts more men. Men pick up on your sexual confidence very strongly and if you are confident in your sexuality, they will notice you more.

Caveat: If you do not enjoy sex, or think that sex is dirty, or feel guilty when you have sex, please do not get a friend with benefits. This advice will not work for you because you do not feel comfortable in your sexuality. Many women, especially those who have been raised in very religious or sexist homes or possibly have been molested, can have very negative feelings about sex. They do not feel empowered in their sexuality. They are not free of the sexist mindset. They often look down on women they deem too "sexual." If you are one of these women I recommend that you do not date but instead take some time to understand your sexual side. This may even require therapy, especially if you have been sexually molested. You will not be able to fully enjoy your dating life if you feel bad or dirty or guilty about your body and sex.

Now that I have told you that your vagina is not your greatest asset please understand that doesn't mean there is not power in your sexuality. Just because sex is not your only asset does not mean it is not an asset. It is just one of your many assets. There is power in your sexuality just as there is power in your intelligence. You have to remember to embrace all of your assets.

Just think about Beyonce. She has completely embraced her sexual side. She is not afraid to flaunt her sexuality. She knows how to capture male attention. She knows how to be sexual and she's powerful as she does it. Not one man can take that power away from her. When it comes to sex, women carry far greater power than men do. This is another reason why men pursue women and not the other way around. They are attracted to that power. This is why men flock to strip clubs and women generally don't. This is also the very reason sexism came about, to control that power. Women knowing they have more power than men in their sexuality means they have the power to control and not the other way around. That is why sexism is so important to keep in place. You can't have a bunch of sexually empowered women running around…men would lose total control...

It is highly important that you are comfortable in your sexual and sensual being. You can use your sexuality and sensuality to attract the men you really are interested in. Embrace your sexuality. Embrace your sensuality. Embrace your womanly power. Don't be afraid to be "sexy." It's empowering.

CHAPTER 7: WHAT YOU CAN LEARN FROM STRIPPERS AND "GROUPIES"

THEY KNOW WHAT MEN WANT

Now that I have told you to let go of sexism's control over your sexuality let's talk about strippers and groupies. You actually can learn a lot from strippers and groupies. Yes, those women with the so called "loose" morals. The women you have been taught to look down on because sexism has told you that women who behave this way are less worthy of respect. Yet, these "less worthy" women are getting all the attention from men that you were taught they don't "deserve." I see it all the time, women upset about so called "hoes winning." This is sexism at work and it's dumb. Why? Because there are some things these women get right when it comes to understanding men.

Why are they perceived as such a threat to "classy" women (besides the fact that some women are looked down on to keep women in control)? It's classic divide and conquer. Strippers and groupies know things about men because they have torn down the "moral" barrier and looked honestly at men to figure out what they really want and how to attract them. They know men really want (you ready?) attention.

WHY MEN LOVE STRIPPERS

Aside from its apparent misogynistic facade, stripping is actually one of the most interesting jobs on the planet. Men pay to see women naked. Think about that for a second. How simple do you have to be to actually pay someone to take their clothes off. That's all strippers have to do, get naked. Now while our male dominated sexist culture makes it seem as though the men are in the dominant position here, think about it again, strippers get paid to take off their clothes. No major skills are required (although some strippers do have major skills, but that's another topic for another day). But, why do men pay to see women naked? What keeps them coming back to strip clubs over and over when they can see naked women for free at home or on the Internet?

Strippers know something most women don't; they know how to create the illusion of interest. Strippers know how to give men the type of attention that caters to a man's ego. (Now this gets even funnier when you find out that a significant number of female strippers are actually gay). They know how to make a man believe they are interested in him to the point they gain his interest and keep it to the point where a man will pay them money to see them over and over again. There are men missing their rent payments because they are so enamored with a stripper. Strippers have mastered the art of giving just the right kind of attention that strokes a man's ego to make him believe she likes him. This attention makes men feel good. Feeling good makes them want to feel that way again and come back for more. It's like a drug. They become addicted to the attention a woman gives them. This is something strippers have mastered, creating the illusion that a man is the only man she is interested in. Strippers do this by just making men feel good about themselves. Strippers know how to make a man feel as if he is the only man in the world. Remember the three basic flirting techniques? Strippers use these, plus more, with mastery. The other big thing strippers have mastered is the art of conversation. One of the biggest things strippers do is talk to men, just talk, not taking off their clothes, but actually just conversing. They have also, of course, totally embraced their sexuality. Basically, strippers know how to use all of their "assets" to gain and keep a man's interest, interest usually, they don't even want.

Embracing all of your assets, intelligence, conversation, flirting, sexuality...and using them as tools in the same way as strippers can help you gain the interest and keep the interest of the man you are attracted to. You don't have to be a stripper and take off your clothes but do take some of their skills as a lesson on how to give men the type of attention they crave. Strippers have men on lock, and that will never change. Make sure you acknowledge their skills instead of looking down on them. See how they too have power, and learn to use some of that power for yourself.

WHY FAMOUS/RICH MEN DATE "GROUPIES"

People really love to trash women who date famous or rich men, and because of sexism, those women are usually called "groupies." But, let's be honest. Women who are called groupies usually get the man they want, and at a much higher frequency than average women. Don't let sexism make you think that groupies are less than you. (Remember divide and conquer)! Why is it that these women seem to attract these famous or rich men at a higher frequency than average women? Is it because of how they look? No. It is because these women, called groupies, understand how to become what they want to attract and like strippers, have mastered using all of their "assets" to attract and keep the attention of the men they want? Now, before you say most groupies are not successful at getting what they want, I want you to understand the differences between women who are actual "groupies" and women who just have groupie aspirations.

Actual "groupies" are not those women you see at the club clamoring over the basketball player that just walked in. In general, the women with the hiked up skirts and cleavage up to their chins standing in line or waiting to be called into VIP are just women with groupie aspirations. They think they have to be "chosen" by the men. They do not understand that women are the choosers. They don't really know how to get the attention of the man they want. They just believe that if they "look" a certain way and act a certain way (often overtly sexual), they will gain the attention of the man they would like to date. Actual "groupies" are not this foolish. Actual "groupies" are at that same club too, but chances are they have their own VIP section. "Why," do you say? Success attracts success. This is why famous or rich men like groupies. The real "groupies" understand that.

While in my twenties I happened to be friends with a woman who many would have considered to be a "groupie." She successfully dated multiple professional football players. She learned her skills from another woman who was married to a baseball player. She broke it down for me one day. She told me how these women study the men they plan to attract. I am probably violating some secret WAG (wives and girlfriends) pact by sharing this information. However, since I am not a WAG I don't feel obligated to stay quiet about these important skills. These women know their "mark." They know where he hangs out, what he likes, and what he dislikes. Groupies take it a step further. Because these men are usually public figures, the women can research his income, assets, and earning potential. One of the things my friend pointed out to me that I had no clue about is that baseball players are preferred by "groupies" because their income is "guaranteed." As she described these techniques to me, in my mind was the question, "Why?" It just seemed to me a lot of work just for a guy. And since dating a professional ball player was never an interest or goal of mine, these techniques seemed crazy.

It was only in recent years that they started to make sense to me. To attract the person you want, you have to know what attracts them to you. Often these women who date famous or rich men have studied the men they want to date, knowing the men's interests, their backgrounds, their likes, and dislikes. They embody the type of woman those men are interested in. Remember when I talked about leagues and circles? Basically, these women have worked their way into the circle they wanted to be in. They have moved into the "league" that has the men they want to date. They know how to present the image that attracts these types of men. They also know where to find the men they are interested in. The women called "groupies" have and use skills that most average women don't. They understand how to project the image needed to get who they want. In other words, they understand that "You are who you attract." These women have "baited their hooks" to catch exactly what they want.

While I would never suggest some of the extremes these women go to to attract famous or rich men, their basic premise is smart. "Be the person you want to attract." For example, a lot of women want to date a rich man. Well, rich men do not want a woman they know they will become financially responsible for. Therefore, being financially independent automatically makes you more attractive to a rich man. This goes back to the discussion on dating leagues. They do exist. If you want to date in a league that you are not currently in, you are going to have to change your league. It's the same thing with dating a smart man; be a smart woman. Groupies figured this out a long time ago. I am sharing this with you, so that you, too, can become what you want to attract.

What if you have your eyes on a particular man? As previously discussed, men go after who they want. If there is a man you are interested in and he has not noticed you, I recommend moving on. However, if you insist on wanting a particular guy, researching him and becoming what he is attracted to can help you. If you do this and he still shows no interest, please understand, you are not his type. Just move on.

Seriously, he is not worth the heartache. (Some of you won't listen anyway but don't say I didn't tell you so).

CHAPTER 8: BUT WHAT ABOUT?

COMPETITION FROM OTHER WOMEN

Sexism has taught women from the time they are little girls to see each other as competition. We are taught this because women united together are very powerful. As long as women are competing with one another sexism maintains its control, especially if we are competing for the affections of a man. That said, you should never see another woman as competition. Women hold much more power together as allies, even in dating. Of course, I know some of you are thinking you have to compete to date. You don't. If a man really wants you, there is no woman that will stop him from dating you. Again, men go after who they really want, and if they do not want you, that's ok too. There is nothing to compete about, (See Chapter 9 "Rejection and Letting Go"). Never feel that you need to compete with other women to get attention from men. If you see a man you are dating out on a date with another woman, say hi. Be confident in who you are. You are free to date multiple people and so is he. The woman he is out with is not your competition. In fact, you should see her as an ally. I have become fast friends with women who dated men that I have also dated. Dating is not a competition. When you connect with someone, you connect. Nothing can come between that connection, not even another woman. Plus, the lack of jealousy and confidence of a woman who is not intimidated or jealous of other women is a quality that men are very attracted to. When you show no signs of jealousy, suddenly men become very curious about why and they will stick around just to figure it out.

But, what if you feel jealous? While everyone has experienced having jealous feelings, it is important to understand that when you feel jealousy it means you are feeling insecure. That has everything to do with you, not the other person. If there is a woman who you happen to find out is dating the same man as you, and you feel jealous, that's a signal to work on yourself, not compete for attention. When you are secure in who you are no person can take that security away from you. No one person is ever a threat to you or your position. Think about it, a woman who is constantly jealous and worried that other women want her boyfriend or husband is that way because she doesn't feel comfortable in her relationship. She is insecure. While sexism has taught us that women can "steal" a man away, that is not possible. Men go willingly to where they want to be. If you feel jealous, that is a signal to do some self-reflection. Do not focus on the person you are jealous of.

INTERNET DATING

Ok, let me be honest, I have never done Internet dating. I have some friends who say it's great and have even found their spouses online. However, I can only speak knowingly on why I choose not to date online.

Online dating takes away the ability for me to gauge whether a man is genuinely interested. Why? Internet dating makes it all too easy for a man to approach a woman. A man taking the time to engage a woman in person to ask her out lets her know he is definitely interested, instead of being only slightly interested. In online dating men see photos of women they find attractive and can just hit a button or swipe and that's it, to let a woman know he's interested. In my opinion, there is no real effort. It's like online shopping, see a woman you like and hit a button to put her in your cart. Because dating is a numbers game men can instantly up their numbers online a lot more easily because they don't have to figure out a way to be engaging. They can just hit a few buttons and boom, another date.

Also, a man's "representative" online can easily be deceptive. People become whoever they want to be online. They become taller, thinner, richer... "Cat fishing" is a very real and huge phenomenon right now in our society. People have a much easier time creating their "representatives" online than they do in person. Both men and women are guilty of this. It is just easier to be the person you want to be instead of the person you actually are online. I have heard multiple stories from men and women who went on a date with someone they met on a dating site who was nothing like the profile they presented. This is not to say that some people are not genuine online, but I am saying that it is a lot more easy to be fake online than in person. When a person is standing in front of you, you can see exactly what they look like. When they talk to you, you can get a lot more information about them than reading their dating profile. Their dating profile is only going to give you the information they want you to know, but when you are in person you have a much greater chance of knowing the things they probably don't exactly want you to know about themselves.

This brings me to my last point about Internet dating. It is much harder to judge the "crazy" in a person when you do it through a computer screen instead of when they are right in front of you. When a man approaches you in person you have more of an opportunity to gauge whether he is mentally stable. It is much easier to determine if someone isn't working with a full deck when you are able to look them in the eye. My preference is to look a man in the eye before deciding whether or not to go out with him. This is just my dating preference. I prefer not to date online. This does not mean that there is anything wrong with dating online. If you apply the same principles in this book to your Internet dating you can still have great results.

USING SOCIAL MEDIA TO YOUR ADVANTAGE

Men are nosy. Believe me, even if they do not follow you on any of your social media accounts, they are still checking them. They can't help it; it's in their nature. That is why it is important that if you have any social media accounts you learn to use them to your advantage when dating. Your social media accounts are part of your appeal. Your social media accounts are your marketing so to speak. For example, at the very moment that I am writing this passage I am on vacation, alone, in Barbados. While here I have been posting pictures on my social media accounts that I took myself with the timer on my camera. The funniest thing about this is, whenever I post these pictures, men flood my phone and inboxes with messages. Why? They think I am here with a man. Their competitive side can't help but react to my illusion of being with another man. Mind you, a good number of these men never hit like on my pictures. Why? Because they do not want the world to know they are watching, but they are. Keep this in mind whenever you post, *the men are watching.*

Learning to use social media so that you present an image of a confident woman who has many options is something you can and should take advantage of. It is your marketing tool. However, many times women make the mistake of using social media to show what they are doing every minute of everyday, or even using social media as a therapy session to air out everything that bothers them. Doing these things can actually hurt your dating life. Again, men are nosy; they are checking out your statuses, every single one. And, if you use social media to constantly complain about your life, they notice. Remember men react to what you put out, so if you are putting out an image of an unhappy person online, men will notice this about you and steer clear. Men see everything you make available for them to see.

One of the biggest mistakes I see women make online is posting pictures with a man they just started dating. Men are waiting for you to post who you are dating. They *love* to see the man who has your attention. They want to know who they are competing with. They want to size him up. Men also know that when you post pictures of your new beau right away you are not secure in the relationship. On top of that, they always notice when you stop dating that guy because (rookie mistake number two) women erase all of the pictures of the guy they were dating from their accounts. Men love when women do this. It's extremely entertaining for them. However, it hurts your dating life. Trust me, when a man likes you he pays attention to everything you do. Therefore, make sure what you put out there is useful to you. Posting pictures with someone who may or may not be around in six months is not helpful for you. Sure take pictures together but keep them in your private collection or share them in your girlfriends' group chat. Be strategic about what you post. This does not mean you can't post freely but every post says something about you. It is your image, your marketing. Make sure your image is one that is attractive.

BEING A MOTHER

I am a mom and I date. Yes, people judge women for being single, especially for being single mothers. If you date, that judgement can sometimes be even more intense. There are looming questions. When are you supposed to let a guy know you are a mom? When should he meet your children? What if he doesn't want children? What if he does? And, of course, what will people say?

Dating while being a mom does not change anything. Seriously. You can date just like a woman without children. You may have more things to consider, such as free time and child care, but your basic dating life is the same as a woman who doesn't have children. You do not have to worry about whether men will like the fact that you have children or not because if they don't like to date women who have children, you should not date them. Problem solved.

Often moms worry about having different men around their children. This apprehension is understandable because sexism gives free rein to those who are inclined to harshly judge what women do. How dare a woman move on after having a child and date *gasp* men. Just look how people treated Ciara when she started dating and then married Russell Wilson. People act as if moving on and dating are wrong for mothers to do, as though the act of dating is damaging to children. What is damaging to children is being raised by an unhappy mother. Your children will always flourish if you are well and happy. In turn, they will suffer if you are unhappy. You have to remember that your happiness affects your children.

Having a good dating life is teaching and reinforcing to your child that happiness is important and healthy companionship is ok. The key to dating while being a mom is being honest with your children about what is going on. I talk to my daughter about the fact that I am going out with a guy and that it does not mean I am going to marry him. I tell her that sometimes people go out and it works out to where they go out again, and also that sometimes it doesn't work out, that it is a part of life. I tell her that if at any point I feel things are going to become more serious with a guy I will let her know. I also assure her that how she feels about someone is extremely important to me. If she doesn't like a guy I am dating that is very important for me to know. I tell her that she should always feel free to tell me what she thinks about someone. I want her to understand that I am not putting anyone before her and that if there are any major life changes she will be informed of them beforehand so that her world will never be suddenly turned upside down. Children need stability; sudden change is usually not good for them. However, children are quite capable of understanding how life works, sometimes more so than adults. Be sure to openly communicate with your child about what is going on in your dating life. This does not mean you have to share details that are not age appropriate. Keep communication open with your children so that they understand what is happening in their world. This is very helpful to them and to you. Also, children sometimes pick up on red flags before we do. Trust your children. If your child reacts badly to a man, leave him alone. Children are very perceptive and smart. If your child doesn't like someone, there is a good chance that person is trying to deceive you. Be open and honest with your children about your dating life. Trust them. Your children have your best interests in mind.

What if you date someone for a while and have to break up? Children often become attached to the same people we become attached to. If you have been dating someone for a while and it doesn't work out, how your child reacts to the breakup truly depends on how much your child has interacted with the man you dated. If your child only knows that you were dating a person, or only met that man a handful of times, then the impact will be minor and you can just inform your child (or not, if the man hasn't really been around much) that you and your friend decided to not date anymore but remain just friends instead. However, if you were deeply involved with a man and your child spent significant time around him, you should take the time to have a conversation explaining why you are no longer dating. You may even want to give your child a chance to talk to the guy you were dating on their own, if they are old enough. Remember, children operate best in an environment of honesty.

Life is not perfect. Letting children understand that relationships can and do end will prepare them for later in life when they may have to face a breakup or divorce themselves. Learning from you how to end a relationship in a healthy way will mean they are more prepared than you probably were. Do not be ashamed to share with your children that a relationship ended. That is a normal part of life.

Also, always be sure to let your children know that even though things did not work out it doesn't mean it is the end of the world and that your family unit will always be in tact. One day there may be a new person added to it, if not, that's ok too. As long as your children know you love them and will be honest with them, they are pretty good about understanding that dating is a normal part of your life. So, go ahead and enjoy your dating life. Your children want to see you happy and they will be happy for you.

Chapter 9: Rejection and Letting Go

Recognizing Rejection

Often when women see the signs of rejection they have a hard time acknowledging and accepting it. This may be because women tend to believe that if a man doesn't want to be with them, it means there is something wrong with them personally, and not simply that the man just isn't interested. In the same way that we women are not interested in every man who crosses our path, men also are not interested in every woman they cross paths with. They also can like someone in the beginning and then later decide they are not interested. It happens. When you notice that a man you were dating slows his normal communication with you, that is a good indication he is no longer interested. In other words if he was calling/texting three times daily and now it's down to once every other day, there is a good chance he wants to move on. He is giving you the "brush off."

If you notice the "brush off" don't go crazy. Do not start calling/texting him more. This is one of the biggest mistakes women make, panicking when a man is no longer interested. *Just relax, it's going to be ok.* I do understand why women sometimes panic when getting the "brush off." Things can be going so well and then all of a sudden the guy we were dating just seems disinterested. Usually when this happens most women just want to know, **"Why?"** Well, it is because most men won't/can't be up front about feeling differently about you. Remember the discussion about men not learning how to express their emotions in a healthy way? Instead of just stating up front that he wants to stop seeing you because he is no longer interested, he will most likely suddenly become "distant." Do not take this personally. Resist the urge to communicate with a man if you do get the "brush off." It will only amplify the rejection in your mind. Just remember, pay attention to the men who pay attention to you. This is the time to focus on yourself. There is nothing bad about rejection. Even though it can hurt, rejection is part of life and many times when we are rejected the circumstances of the rejection end up in our favor.

Very often being rejected can push you into a more powerful direction. Rejections are life's little jolts to "wake us" up. Sometimes rejection can cause you to reevaluate yourself or your circumstances. Sometimes rejection can cause you to decide to work on personal pursuits you wouldn't have if you had not been rejected. Sometimes a rejection will make you decide to make a complete lifestyle change. Anything that causes self-growth is a good thing. So, instead of looking at rejection as a loss or defeat, accept rejection as a push towards a better direction for yourself. Just keep moving forward, better things are always on the horizon. Remember, there are a lot of men in the world. If one doesn't like you, there are thousands more who will. Keep it moving.

LETTING GO

A lot of times women meet a guy and he just seems so "perfect" in our minds despite the multiple red flags. We will ignore the red flags and get "stuck on stupid" for him because we become strangely and strongly attached to him. What causes this I am not sure. Not only have I witnessed it with multiple friends, but have been guilty of it myself; I am speaking from a place of experience. Sometimes the man you like or love the most is the one person you need to leave alone because he is simply not good for you. Women tend to think of themselves last when it comes to mental and emotional health, however, someone who keeps you in a place of unhappiness and confusion is a person who is not good for you. You need to let him go.

When you are dealing with a man who isn't good for you, letting go of him is the best thing you can do for yourself. It is always important to maintain control of your life and keep your "power." When we refuse to let go we give our power to the other person. They then have the ability to keep us in an unhappy place because we refuse to let them go. In addition, it is important to remember that the person who lets go first will always be in the power position later. I say this because many times women will keep hoping for a dating situation to turn into a relationship or for a relationship to continue because they just do not want to let go. The longer you hold on to a guy who is not good for you the more you allow the man to hold power over you. Not letting go makes it even harder for you to move on when you most need to. We all can form deep attachments to people, but sometimes for our own benefit we need to let go of these attachments and trust that if it is meant to be, it will happen in its right time.

If you are able to cut a man off, totally and completely, meaning you stop all communication, no calls, no texts, no emails, nothing, you will always hold the power position if he tries to come back. The truth is, if a man was ever into you, he will always come back, it can be a week, a month, a year, ten years, men will always come back. One more time so you understand, it's ok to let go because **men always come back**. Even a man my mother dated decades ago tried to reconnect with her this year (she politely let him know she was not interested). Why? Because men always come back if they were really into you, especially when you let them go. Never be afraid to let go of a situation that isn't working out. When you do, if it is meant to be, he will be back. Just so you know, most of the time when a man does come back into your life, your life has grown and changed so much that you do not even want him anymore. Never be afraid to let go.

I do understand that letting go can be difficult. Attachment is comforting. People always get comfortable with what is familiar and dating someone is one of the most familiar situations you can be in. It can sometimes take months to let go because going back to what is comfortable is always tempting. However remember, no one has ever grown from being comfortable. Self-growth comes from pushing through the uncomfortable times. When faced with a situation where you know you should let a guy go, do it. Do not be afraid. That means resist the urge to call/text/email/Facebook/SnapChat…etc. I know it is hard, but the more disciplined you are at letting go, and cutting off all communication, the better you will get at it. Plus, there will always be more men to date. In fact, going on another date is a very good way to let go. Remember, pay attention to the men who pay attention to you.

GETTING RID OF THE "DICK RESIDUE"

You need to let the "dick residue" wear off. If you are one of my girls I may have said this to you at one time or another when you were dealing with a guy you shouldn't have. While I always said it in jest, the truth is we all have a much harder time letting go of a guy we should let go of when we don't stop having sex with him. Why? Hormones make us make bad decisions. "Dick residue" as I like to call it, is the "sex haze" we get after having sex with a guy we really like. You will always feel "lovey dovey" after you have sex with him making it that much harder to let go when you need to. One of the biggest mistakes women make is turning the guy they should leave alone into the "friend with benefits." This never works. I always tell my girlfriends when they are caught up with a guy they should let go of, to stop having sex with him so the "dick residue" can wear off. Once that "residue" wears off you will be able to make a clear decision for yourself. Usually that decision involves moving on. However, you cannot move on until you get all the "residue" off of you. Make sure you cut the sex off so you can see clearly again, because "residue" will always "cloud" your judgement.

Chapter 10: Understanding Love

Love is selfless

Love, real love, is one of the hardest things for people to understand. It is one of the emotions we are least exposed to in this world. Outside of our parents' love, we rarely see it. Romantic love is taught to us as something that real love isn't. We think love is some crazy feeling that sweeps us up and makes our brains go fuzzy. Love in books, movies, and tv shows is something that is romanticized, but it is not actually what real love is.

Love, real love, is selfless, meaning you give your love freely to the person you love without any expectations in return. This concept is not what our society traditionally teaches about love. We are so used to thinking that love means two people who belong to one another, that one is in the possession of another. Love is not possession. While many people believe that is what love is, that is not love. When you truly love someone you can love them from afar. (Sometimes that is the best thing that can happen). When you truly love someone, with real love, you will love them whether you are in a relationship with them or not. Your love for a person does not change based on how they treat you, you simply love them as they are. Many times people think that because they are physically attracted to someone they love them. Love has nothing to do with sex. Love is not lust.

Most of the time when we think we love someone we expect something in return, usually things or actions, but something is always expected. To really understand dating and to really manage your dating expectations you really need to understand what love is. It is selfless. Love probably does exist in some form between most people who choose to be together but it is probably not love in its truest form. Love in its truest sense means loving someone without any expectation of return. And, let's be honest. Most people are not able to selflessly love anyone else other than our children, (and some people aren't even capable of that).

Well then, what is that "lovey dovey" feeling you get when you connect with someone new? That's hormones and very similar to a drug high. Your brain is releasing chemicals to help you bond with someone. Humans do bond. New mothers experience an influx of hormones after giving birth to help her bond to her newborn. You are experiencing this influx of hormones when you first date someone. You should enjoy the feeling, but recognize it for what it is, a temporary high. There are some couples who have learned to make this mental high last forever but most of the time it is temporary. The fact that it is temporary is not a bad thing. If you made it to the point where you have the "lovey dovey" feelings for someone and you have taken the time to get to know them, you may even reach the point where you find that there is compatibility between the two of you. Compatibility is ultimately what you need to continue a bond with someone. Incompatibility breaks up relationships and marriages all the time. Sometimes the incompatibility happens because one or both of the people changed in some way. Most of the time the incompatibility was there in the beginning and one or both of the people involved chose to ignore it. I know that this book is about dating but it is important that I touch on the fact that you can actually find love while you are out there dating. I want you to be able to recognize it if it happens.

You may also end up loving a guy who is not "good for you." I want to point out that it is quite possible to love a man but not be in a relationship with him, especially if he is not good for you. See love for what it is, selfless. You can love someone selflessly without being in a relationship with him. This is important to remember. Many women will get involved and even stay involved with a man all while sacrificing her own happiness and her life, just because she believes that she "loves" him. While in the beginning she may be able to live with this type of sacrifice, eventually this type of relationship, doing what she thinks she should do because she "loves" him, will lead her to a depressed life. What you do not want to do is sacrifice your happiness, your life, because you love someone who is not good for you. Usually in these types of relationships the man does not selflessly love you back. Basically, the woman is selflessly loving someone at the sacrifice of herself. This is never healthy. That is why it is so important to understand that you can love a man and not be in a relationship with him. Always take care of yourself. Do not sacrifice yourself just to be in a relationship. You are worth more than that.

But, what if you feel like you cannot live without a particular man. You feel you need this man to function, that your life has no meaning unless this man is in it. **That isn't real love.** That is a combination of hormones, insecurities, and possibly manipulation. That is your desire to possess that person for your own needs. You should never feel as though you cannot live without someone. Yes, you may feel that you never want to be without them, but you should always feel that you can live without them if need be. Think about our previous discussion on how our society has taught us to believe that certain manipulative behaviors make us believe that we are in love and then remember, love is selfless. Love is not pain.

A lot of people believe if you aren't in pain over a person then you are not really in love. The truth is love should never hurt. If you are in pain over a man, that is usually a big sign that you are being manipulated. Make sure that you are not involved with someone who is exhibiting the emotionally manipulative behaviors that I talked about in Chapter 5. Love should always make you feel good. When you are in a situation of real love you do not experience pain. This does not mean that you will never have a disagreement or argument or hard times. It means that at your core the love you have for one another strengthens you. Love should always feel good, never painful. When you are in a relationship where you both share a real love for one another, you will always feel empowered in your relationship, never unsure, insecure, or jealous. Remember not to confuse manipulation with actual love. If you are involved with a man and you find yourself confused, unsure, insecure, or hurt, you are not in love. You are in pain. And, you are dating someone who is not good for you.

Remember as you navigate the dating world, date men who are "good for you." Let go of situations that hurt you or that make you feel unsure or insecure. There is nothing to be gained from them. You are not being loved and you are not in love. Make sure you understand that there are always more men to date. Always. Never get hung up on someone who causes you pain when there are many more who can bring you joy. If it is not working out, keep it moving!

Final Thoughts

There you have it, my approach to dating, as unconventional as it may seem. Some will cheer what I have shared while others will get their "knickers in a knot." Regardless of whether you like or hate this book, I hope ultimately it will help you to become happier. Even if it helps just one person, I have reached my goal. Always remember, life will go on and something beautiful is there waiting just for you.

Acknowledgements

To my beautiful family, especially my mother and daughter, thank you for allowing me the time to write this book and especially for helping me with all the other things that needed to be done. I would not have been able to complete this if it were not for you two. You kept our household together while I took time to focus on writing.

Mommy, you have always been there as my rock. I would not be who I am without you. You have been there for me no matter the challenges. I know that I would not have made it through this life without you. I am eternally grateful to have such a strong, smart, beautiful, and inspiring woman in my life; not everyone is as fortunate to have a mother like you. I feel very lucky.

Little Flower, you inspire me to be better every day. From the moment you came into my life you changed me for the better. You gave me purpose I never knew I had. You make me want to do more and more good in the world. Motherhood for me was transformative; I feel extremely lucky to be your mommy. I look forward to seeing the woman you will become. I knew from the moment you got here that you were very special. I am happy that I have the opportunity to see you grow each and every day. Thank you for being the sweet, caring, beautiful, and funny person that you are.

My endless list of friends, I love you all and I am thankful for every experience we have shared. Some of those experiences even ended up in this book! (Lol)! Thanks for the support; thank you for the friendship, and especially thank you for the laughs.

To my Twitter peeps, thank you. Especially you, Napoleon Harrington (@NHarringtonJr). Your gentle prodding and encouragement over the years kept me working on this book. For that I am very grateful.

And last but not least, to my "#1 Fan" (you know exactly who you are). Thank you!

END NOTES

QUOTED MATERIAL

Page 36
"He's just not that into you." - "Pick-A-Little, Talk-A-Little." *Sex and the City.* HBO. July 13, 2003. Television.

Page 79
"[A]ccording to research, the average married woman is less happy than the average married man, less happy than single women, less convinced that married people are happier than single people, and more likely to file for divorce. Once returned to single life, women's happiness recovers, whereas men's declines, and divorced women are less eager to remarry than divorced men." - Wade, Lisa. (2017, January 10). *The Modern Marriage Trap — and What to Do About It.* http://time.com/money/4630251/the-modern-marriage-trap-and-what-to-do-about-it/

Page 99

"[Women] consistently underestimate ourselves. Multiple studies in multiple industries show that women often judge their own performance as worse than it actually is, while men judge their own performance as better than it actually is." - Sandberg, Sheryl. *Lean In*. New York. Alfred A. Knopf, 2013. Print.

Page 101

"[I]nfant boys are more emotionally reactive than girls. They display more positive as well as negative affect, focus more on the mother, and display more . . . distress and demands for contact than do girls." - Kraemer, Sebastian. "The Fragile Male." BMJ: British Medical Journal 321.7276 (2000): 1609–1612. Print.

About The Author

Kai Nicole holds degrees from Harvard University and Howard University School of Law.

She has worked in law, entertainment, technology (Silicon Valley), and has done business development consulting for multiple entrepreneurs.

A native Washingtonian, she has also lived in Boston and Atlanta. Kai is currently residing with her family in the suburbs of San Francisco.

Website: www.DateLikeAWoman.com

DLAW
P.O. Box 1445
Pacifica, CA 94044-2009